Get Coaching Now!

The How, What and Why of Effective Pet Industry Client Consultations - *Featuring On Task Skill Coaching*™

By Niki Tudge
© Copyright 2017

Contents

Introduction   iv

    The Strategic Model for On Task Skill Coaching   viii

The Approach   1

    The Consultation and Functional Assessment   1
    The Informant Interview   11
    The Direct Observation   16
    The Functional Analysis   22
    Using Logic and Critical Thinking   26
    Establishing the Voice of the Customer   28

The Planning   33

    The Training/Behavior Change Program   34
    How Will the Plan Look?   35
    Key Question   36
    Systematic Desensitization and Counterconditioning   39
    A Sample Outline of a Behavior Change Case
    - Separation Anxiety   42
    A Sample Outline of a Training Situation
    – Teaching a Dog to Sit   46

Behavior Change, Training or Management?	49
Management Only	49
Training Programs	50
Behavior Change Programs	51
Skill Gap Analysis - Baseline Measurements	52

The Environment — 54

Creating Connections between Learning and Memory	54
Environmental Pressure	56
Coaching for Results	59
Motivation	*60*
Create a Trusting Environment	62

The System - On Task Skill Coaching — 65

The On Task Skill Coaching Method	69
The Road Map	71
The Training Lesson Plan	**73**
Teaching versus Training	76
The Individual Sessions	79
Quick Preparation Checklist	81
Step 1: Open the Session	86
Step 2: Show the Finished Skill	90
Step 3: The One-Way Demo	92
Step 4: The Two-Way Demo	92
The "How" Explained	94
Step 5: Trainee Performs the Task	95
Step 6: Supervised Practice	98

Step 7: Wrap Up the Session	98
Step 8: Assign Homework	99
Implementation	100
References	105

Introduction

I have been involved in small business consulting across the pet industry for many years. I have also owned and operated several pet businesses, with gross operating incomes ranging from US $100,000 to $500,000 per year. I have made a common observation in each of these businesses, whether it was an animal hospital, a boarding facility, or an in-home dog training and pet care service company: The professionals who own and work within small pet-related businesses often seem to display a distinct lack of formalized people training skills.

It is thus my belief that there is a lack of competent people training skills across the pet industry, and that this deficit is largely responsible for many of the issues that commonly plague professional individuals and their businesses. I outline some of them on the following page. All things being equal, if one has all the necessary attending expertise and behavioral analytical skills within the scope of pet dog training yet is still experiencing issues within one's business, I hypothesize it is related directly to one's ability to train, coach and mentor people. These are skills that do not always come naturally and, consequently, require some additional education and adult learning. Some people are lucky to have natural leadership skills, but refined communication skills and management skills are usually learned in a formal setting.

As professionals, we need to ask ourselves if we can relate to one or more of the following problems within our businesses:

- Difficulty in converting prospects to customers.
- Private training clients who start out "gung ho" and then fall off the program prior to achieving their goals.
- Pet care clients who disregard our advice.
- Substantial group class attrition.
- Time expended trying to convince clients, rather than teach them.
- Frustrated clients who appear to just "not get it."
- Lack of client knowledge retention across our training services.
- An apparent lack of client commitment to our methods and suggested ideas.
- Incomplete homework assignments and insufficient practice of skills.
- Difficulty and frustration engaging clients and changing their attitudes so we can build consensus and support their needs.

In our roles as training and behavior experts, we are both teachers and trainers. We have a unique role to play when clients seek our help and expertise. Irrespective of how competent we are at our craft or how much knowledge we have, if we cannot adequately impart this onto our clients, then we are doing them a disservice.

In the fields of animal training and behavior, it is widely

accepted that it is unlikely, if not impossible, to be fully competent across all the varied industry services. As a result, some professionals elect to be very strategic when defining their scope, and narrow their focus to areas they both enjoy and feel competent in. From a marketing perspective, selecting limited services and marketing oneself as an expert in a specific niche can be a strategically savvy move. It is critical that, as professionals, we recognize and acknowledge our own competent skill set and work within its confines. Regardless, whether we choose to focus on a specific type of training, a specific protocol, or pet care services, the one very important skill we all need is the ability to teach people to train and care for their own animals.

Potential Service Offerings
- ✓ Private In-Home Training
- ✓ Board & Train Programs
- ✓ One-on-One Training
- ✓ Behavior Consultations
- ✓ Aggression Consultations
- ✓ Group Class Training
- ✓ Puppy Training
- ✓ Day Training
- ✓ Separation Anxiety
- ✓ Resource Guarding

Research proposes that people in training or teaching roles tend to implement the same teaching method they experienced as students. In the absence of a training certification program that focuses on teaching skills rather than just the transfer of knowledge, this means that, if most of an individual's learning experience was lecture-based, for example, then that probably forms the foundation of how that individual now teaches their students (Wolvin, 1983).

Lecturing students is regarded as an easy and convenient method of teaching. Indeed, it is a constructive model for communicating conceptual knowledge, particularly when there is a significant knowledge gap between the teacher and the students, and when there is a large audience. During lectures, the teacher only has to focus on covering his or her program content and not on whether the student is learning anything or not. This type of teaching has been in play for over 800 years and remains a traditional method for many universities. Lecturing was, of course, the teaching method of choice and even necessity prior to the inception of text books. A convenient concept, lecturing is entrenched into our system of knowledge dissemination. However, as is often the case, what is convenient is not always the most effective option.

Experiential learning, the science behind the On Task Skill Coaching™ discussed in this book, is an adult-centric learning process whereby students develop skills and knowledge from direct experiences rather than in traditional classrooms or academic settings. In dog trainer speak, this means no more lectures or one-way-training traffic, but an integrated approach using the learning cycle and a process-driven system that works.

As pet professionals, we need to look at and be prepared to change how we deliver the necessary information to our clients, whether it is for the teaching of new skills or the active engagement of differing philosophies and methods. Even for simple tasks like fitting a harness, trimming nails, or playing fetch, specific skills are still required for them to be done correctly. An experience is an osmosis of action and thought and is the bridge that connects students to whatever object they are interacting with. When we experience something, we do not separate the action from the end result. Each complements the other on a loop system and new experiences, when mastered, become the foundation to the new learning experience. To this end, I present the Strategic Model for On Task Skill Coaching™ (*see Figure 1-1*). I hope you will find this helpful in your training and teaching roles.

Introduction

Figure 1-1: The Strategic Model for On Task Skill Coaching™

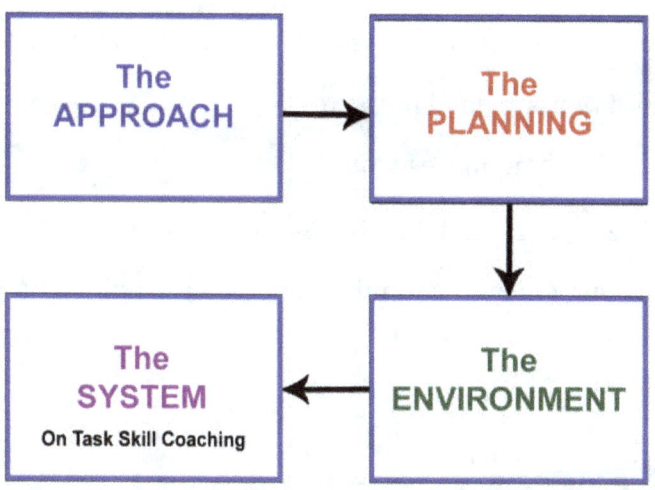

The Strategic Model for On Task Skill Coaching

The strategic model for On Task Skill Coaching contains four components:

1. **The Approach**

    a. The client consultation – the project definition, scope and goals, and the functional assessment of the problem behavior.

    b. Establishing the voice of the customer, and

    c. critical to quality components.

2. **The Planning**

    a. What the plan will look like.

    b. Whether the plan will involve management, training, behavior change, or a combination.

c. Determining the skill gap analysis.

3. **The Environment**

   a. Creating connections between learning and memory.

   b. Environmental pressure.

   c. Coaching for results.

4. **The System – The Tactical Component**

   a. Implement the training (the On Task Skill Coaching system).

   b. The road map.

   c. The lesson plan.

   d. The sessions.

   e. The what, how and why.

   f. Effective demonstrations.

   g. Student practice.

   h. Review.

   i. Bringing it all together.

We will now look at each of these four steps in more detail to help us understand what is required from each one, and how to ensure the strategic On Task Skill Coaching™ system can function at its best under our direction.

The Approach

The Consultation and Functional Assessment

The approach stage of On Task Skill Coaching defines our project. This is where we must understand the exact nature of the project's scope, as well as determine what is included and what is not. A key part of this is to complete a functional assessment and attain the voice of the customer, i.e. a client's opinion on what it is critical to achieve for the program to be successful. It is also important to set the stage and formalize the consulting relationship with clients.

When we start a consulting or training relationship, we should first ensure we have a contract with the client. As professionals working with animals, there are multiple liability risks open to us. Most of these will stem from one of three areas. Firstly, if, as trainers, we are negligent and do not take reasonable measures to prevent a foreseeable injury from occurring during our contract period, then we are liable. Secondly, we can be found liable if we violate any public safety laws or, thirdly, if we misrepresent our skills or knowledge to a client.

There are a few steps we can take to limit the risk of liability. To start with, we must ensure we have the correct insurance coverage with a reputable company that specializes in the fields of animal training, behavior and pet care. Also, we must always be careful when choosing our working locations and ensure they are safe from potential hazards. Finally, we must take into consideration the movement of the dogs we are going to see, i.e. how will they access and leave the area, is there appropriate fencing, doorways, access to and from parking areas, and areas where there may be other people? Professionals must take into consideration the risk factors presented by each individual dog's behavior. Is the dog aggressive? Is there a bite or fight history? Is there any flight risk? What other concerns are there?

We must adhere to all county, state and federal laws at all times, as must all other persons concerned with the dog's behavior. Each involved person must have signed a consulting contract that covers the liability statements, which should include a liability and limits liability, a liability waiver, and an indemnification policy.

We should only consult within the range of our competency and, if necessary, refer clients to another professional who can better serve their needs. At the end of each consulting contract we should confirm to clients – in writing – a summary of the training, the progress made during the session, and any training, management or safety recommendations we have made for the future welfare of the pet and his/her family. If we have any concerns regarding the pet, then we should document those too at this time.

We must also inform clients that, as pet guardians and owners, they are liable for damage caused by their dogs and open to liability risks if their dog's behavior results in injury or damage to another person, pet or property. Always have clients check with their local authorities, as these liabilities differ from state to state and county to county. Make sure you are familiar with your own state laws and know where to direct clients for more information.

Some states operate with a strict statutory system where pet owners are responsible for all damages, irrespective of whether negligence is proven or not. In states that operate under the one-bite rule, dog owners are responsible for damages after the first bite. Owners need to be particularly cognizant of their liability if they are working with or managing a dog with aggression issues. We need to educate our clients on the importance of having strategies to manage and implement the necessary safety protocols at home, in the yard and whenever they leave home.

The formal contract is not the end of the professional-client contract story, however. Once we have established that our contract and liability waiver have been understood and signed, we must then consider the psychological contract. In short, this summarizes the beliefs held by both trainer and student regarding what they expect from one another. It is an unwritten set of expectations constantly at play during the term of the formal contract. The interactions we have with our clients are a fundamental feature of the trainer-student relationship. Each role is a set of behavioral expectations that are often explicit and not defined in the business contract (Armstrong, 2003).

Armstrong (2003) states that the psychological contract is blurred at the edges, cannot be enforced by either party and is most often not written down. Yet this contract guides expectations, defines roles and helps interpret the relationship between the two parties. It creates emotions that form and control participants' behavior (*see Figure 1- 2*). The essence of the psychological contract is a system of beliefs that needs to be articulated to the client (*see *page 5 for examples of topics discussed during this session).*

In the absence of a mutual understanding of this contract, one side of the equation is most likely going to feel disappointed or let down at some point. This is one of the first things to take care of when beginning a trainer-student relationship. Let us start by setting the scene:

- I have handled my initial sales inquiry professionally and have formalized a consulting appointment.
- My client has completed my online behavior consultation form, which includes all the information I need to prepare for my first meeting safely and competently.
- My contract terms have been communicated, shared and signed and I am in receipt of my first appointment payment.
- I have attended the first consultation, conducted my functional assessment and developed a working hypothesis. I have a contingency statement describing what I believe, with a high rate of confidence, is eliciting the problematic behavior and/or maintaining it.

I am beginning to formulate in my mind which of the following options to implement when going forward:

- A management plan.
- A training plan.
- A complete behavior change program.
- A combination of one or more of the above.

The family are still operating at novice level. They do not know what they do not know. They are unconsciously incompetent.

The Approach

All is well and they are feeling good. The expert is on site and their problems are going to be fixed.

Now it is time for real discussions and contract agreements. I call this our "creating shared meaning" session. How this goes and how effective I am will determine the successful outcome of our team efforts, and is critical to the success of the training program. Not only does it remove any ambiguity surrounding the relationship and the future, but also creates a due north for how we move forwards together as a team.

Figure 1-2: Expectations of the Psychological Contract for Trainers and Clients

Psychological Contract – Client Point of View	Psychological Contract – Trainer Point of View
• The trainer will treat them fairly, respectfully and consistently. • They will obtain a clear understanding of the scope of the work, time investment and reliability of the trainer. • They will understand how much involvement and influence they will have in the process. • They will trust in the trainer to keep his/her word. • They will trust that the trainer will provide a safe working and learning environment. • They will understand role delineation between all parties.	• The client will make an effort throughout the relationship. • The client will be compliant. • The client will be committed. • The client will be loyal to the cause and to their pet(s) during the program.

What is discussed during this creating shared meaning session?

I am very open with my clients and always highlight the need for complete transparency. I explain how I am going to share with them everything they need to know upfront so they can offer informed consent and agree to our plan of action. We are going to discuss each point and clarify anything that is unclear. We are going to put ourselves in a situation where, as from today, we operate as a team and make no assumptions about the journey we are starting. The points we discuss are:

- My role versus their role - who has responsibility for training and caring for the pet, and who is responsible for the training and care of the client.

- What will be expected in terms of time commitment and effort from each member of the family, and how are we going to make this fun and empowering?

- What will each session look like, how will the client experience it, how will the training sessions move forward, and what will each person's role be in these sessions?

- The specifics of all management activities that will need to be incorporated into the family's schedule.

- The specifics of all relationship-building activities that will need to be incorporated into the family's schedule.

- The specifics of all exercise sessions that will need to be incorporated into the family's schedule.

- Safety concerns (if necessary). We make commitments regarding how things will be managed and whose role the specific management tasks are.

- The training protocols, the philosophy and how things will work. We do not judge or criticize anything the client has previously attempted. We are there to make progress and focus on the future not to assign blame for the past.

- What is in it for each person - we begin to create a vision for change, a vision that each member of the family wants to help create.

In summary, the psychological contract refers to the unwritten set of expectations of the consulting relationship. Taken together, the psychological contract and the business contract define the consultant-client relationship.

Now all of this has taken place, we can begin to look at the case in front of us and how we can best find solutions

At the onset of any client-consultant relationship, we already know that behavior is lawful and a product of its environment. Respondent behavior is controlled by antecedent stimuli, and operant behavior is controlled by both antecedent and postcedent stimuli in the three-term contingency. The primary purpose of a functional assessment is to "identify the function of the problem behavior," and what it serves to achieve (Miltenberger, 2004, p. 261). We cannot proceed and develop solutions if we do not really understand how the behavior interacts with the environment. Nor can we functionally change the behavior without changing the antecedent arrangement or the postcedent package, i.e. the consequences.

As professionals, we ideally need to take a strategic approach to behavior consulting. It is a project and needs to be managed accordingly, making the best use of the resources available. It is also important to understand the models available for analyzing behavior and the differences between them.

There are three key approaches to understanding and changing behavior.

a. *The Ethological Model*. This works at the species level of behavior to analyze the relationship between the animal's environment and his adapted genes.

b. *The Medical Model*. This approach diagnoses and treats a behavior problem like an illness or disease. The problem behavior is then categorized and a veterinarian prescribes set protocols. The medical model does not analyze the cause of the behavior or look at the specifics of the individual animal with the problematic behavior. Instead, it addresses the problem behavior through surgery, pharmacological intervention, or anecdotal explanations based on what the behavior looks like, or what is believed to be the animal's psychological condition. These protocols and prescribed treatments are based on intuition and passed-down medical protocols.

> **Important:** *Complicated behavior change cases will need the collaboration and intervention of a veterinary behaviorist, who will work within both the medical and behavior analytical model having the skills and knowledge to support behavior change with pharmaceutical intervention to help bridge and expedite a training and behavior plan.*

The Behavior Analytical Approach. Unlike the previous two

models, this approach recognizes that behavior is a product of the environment and each individual animal's conditioning history. This approach is very analytical and accepts that, in order to change the problem behavior, the underlying causes need to be identified. The approach focuses on the details of the specific behavior and not how the behavior evolved or what physiological processes are driving it. With serious cases that involve anxiety, fear or aggression, the medical model is often necessary, so a training or behavior change program can be implemented effectively.

The behavior analytical approach is far more effective, and certainly more efficient than the medical model alone, because it is based on the sciences of learning and behavior, and follows scientific processes to identify the antecedents and consequences of any given behavior. This approach also avoids relying on guesswork, trial and error tactics, or anecdotal recommendations.

There are three recognized methods for functionally assessing behavior: the indirect observation method, the direct observation method, and the experiential method. This behavior analytical approach is called a functional assessment (*see Figure 1-3*), and it systematically identifies the functional relationship between the behavior and the environment (Miltenberger, 2004). Only when this relationship has been identified can efficient and effective solutions be developed and implemented. As an example, we cannot countercondition a problematic stimulus unless we know precisely what that stimulus is, and under what conditions it elicits the problematic behavior. Thus, before we can begin to teach our human clients to train their dogs, we need to have a specific plan of action in terms of what we are going to train. We must be cognizant of what skills are required, and what knowledge the owner needs to support the skill training. This plan is based on the output of the functional assessment and the goals of the client.

> **Important:** *The process of conducting a functional assessment is a systematic process for approaching behavior change programs.*

In some cases, it will only be necessary to use one or two of the methods to examine the functional relationships. With more complicated behavior problems, and when multiple contingencies are occurring, it will also be necessary to conduct a functional analysis of the behavior.

The first part of functionally assessing behavior is by way of an informant interview, which is where anecdotal information about the problem behavior is sourced. The informant interview is considered an indirect observation method as it uses questioning and questionnaires to capture and gather data. Next, the direct observation process occurs when behavior is observed, and the relationship between the variables is measured and correlated. During this process, the consultant observes the behavior and records important data. The functional analysis is the last part of the process, where relationships between the behavior and its environment are tested.

The Approach

Figure 1-3: The Three Ways to Functionally Assess Behavior

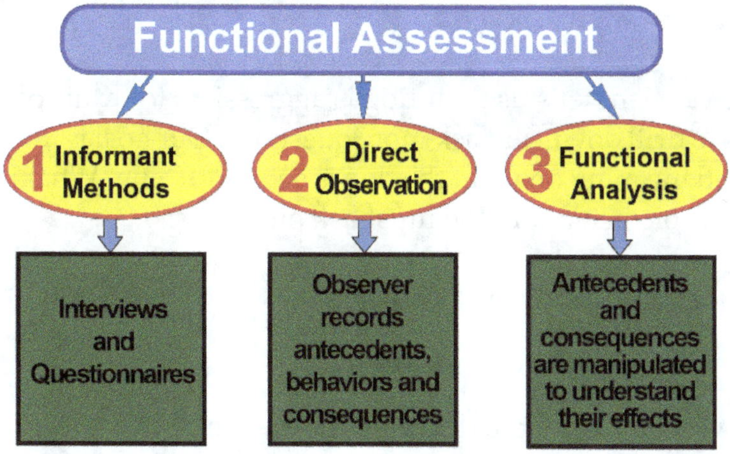

Functional Assessment

1. **Informant Methods** → Interviews and Questionnaires
2. **Direct Observation** → Observer records antecedents, behaviors and consequences
3. **Functional Analysis** → Antecedents and consequences are manipulated to understand their effects

We will now look at each stage in more detail.

The Informant Interview

The goal of the interview process is for pet professionals to collect information from the animal's guardian(s), which will assist in developing a contingency statement of what is happening when the pet engages in the problem behavior.

During the interview, we must be aware that answers provided by the pet owner are often interpretations of behavior, and should thus be considered labels. We need to ask incisive questions and convert the answers into clear descriptions of the actual observable and quantifiable behavior. We must also filter through all the constructs and labels provided by the anecdotal evidence, and establish what is really happening. What is the actual behavior, what is the intensity, the duration, the frequency, the latency? The behavior must be described in objective terms as opposed to subjective labels.

Clients may be very emotional when they talk to us about their pets, and often the information they give us is shrouded in cultural myths.

When a client tells us their dog is aggressive, for example, we have to drill down and ask more questions. Our goal is to create shared meaning on what the dog is actually doing. What is the observable behavior? We must ask ourselves:

- What exactly are we seeing?
- How is the body posture?
- Where does the dog position his weight?
- What facial expressions do we see?
- What is the position of the dog's mouth?
- How vocal is the dog? It is helpful to describe what he sounds like.
- How intense is the behavior, and how much energy is the dog putting into the behavior?
- How long does the behavior last, and why does it stop?

Important: Informant Interview = Anecdotal Evidence
Anecdotal evidence is first- or second-hand information about an individual's personal experience. Both positive and negative anecdotal evidence are unreliable as they do not provide tangible data that can be stratified, analyzed or scientifically interpreted.
(Chance, 2008, p. 42).

The Approach

During the informant interview, there are several components of information that need to be gathered. This data can be collected across group headings on an informant interview questionnaire.

Examples of required question groupings include:

- History - training, background, source, or provider.
- Health – vaccinations, ongoing medical issues, historical issues.
- Exercise - daily, type, play, quantity, with whom.
- Living conditions - home size, crating, family members, other pets, length of time left alone.
- Training history - a detailed history of when, what type, and how effective any training has been.
- Management history - any management activities that are in place now based on the behavioral issue, and the success or failure of any management protocols.
- Behavioral history - when it started, what it is in measurable terms, setting events, motivating operations, antecedents, and consequences.
- Client goal - what the client hopes to achieve from the behavior consultation. What does success look like?

Throughout the client interview process, we must develop a clear, concise, measurable description of the problem behavior(s). It is important to understand the setting events and contexts that make the behavior more likely. It is also necessary to understand the motivating operations, the stimuli that influence the value of the consequences such as satiation or deprivation, and any conditioned emotional responses, such as fear or aggression. (*See below for a broader definition of setting events, motivating operations and emotional responses*).

Important: Distant Antecedents

Setting Events *provide a context and influence target behaviors. (O'Heare, 2007, p. 320).*

Motivating Operations *affect and influence the value of the reinforcer and therefore increase or decrease the likelihood of the discriminative stimulus to evoke the behavior. (O'Heare, 2007, p 320).*

Emotional Responses *motivate a measurable operant behavior, because they do so in this way then they are considered to "serve as motivating operations." (O'Heare, 2007, p. 229).*

It is important to note that behavior never happens in a vacuum, making it necessary to understand the conditions that set the context for any given behavior. We need to precisely identify any eliciting stimuli, as well as the consequences of the behavior. In order to understand why a pet is exhibiting a specific behavior, we need to be able to answer a number of questions. What does the pet get out of this situation? What is he trying to access or what is he trying to avoid? Why is this behavior working for him?

As consultants, we need to rate the efficiency of the problematic behavior, particularly if there are several behaviors at play. In many cases, there are multiple contingencies occurring at the same time, and we need to keep peeling back the layers until we really understand what is going on. The history of the behavior should be sought from the client and the results, if any, from previous behavioral change programs documented.

During the interview, it is also necessary to determine what alternative behaviors the pet's owner(s) would feel are more appropriate and acceptable so that mutually agreeable goals can be set. As we know, sometimes clients have very unrealistic goals. It is our role, however, to help them develop achievable goals that all family members can accept and stand by. At the close of the informant interview, the consultant may be able to develop a contingency statement, i.e. a "what/if" statement.

Important: What is a Contingency Statement?

Behavioral contingencies state the if-then conditions that set the occasion for the potential occurrence of certain behavior and its consequences.

It helps when developing the contingency statement to begin by identifying the B (the behavior). For example, we would not state "aggression" as this is a label only. We would state what is actually happening, e.g. barking, growling, and/or lunging. Then we complete the A (the antecedent, or what comes before the behavior). Finally, we fill in the C (the consequence, or what happens directly after the behavior). We believe the C has a functional relationship with the behavior, and is what is reinforcing the behavior.

A sample contingency statement may look like the one below, in which the antecedent is a stranger approaching a dog who is out on a walk with his owner. Another contingency statement will most likely look very different, and may not include the antecedent or the consequences (if these were not revealed during the informant interview).

Distant Antecedents: Dog is on a walk with his owner (context).

Antecedent: Not sure.

Behavior: Barking, growling, and lunging.

Consequence: Negative reinforcement.

Prediction: The behavior will continue as it is being reinforced through the avoidance of a negative outcome and/or the removal of an aversive (to the dog) stimulus.

The Direct Observation

In many cases where simple behavior challenges are involved, the informant interview will be enough to develop a reliable contingency statement. If, however, at the close of the interview we do not have a high level of comfort with our contingency statement, or cannot develop a hypothesis from the anecdotal data we have gathered, then it is time to move onto step two, the direct observation.

The goal of the direct observation is to pinpoint the source of the problem by factually understanding the functional relationships between the antecedents, the behavior and the consequence(s).

The process facilitates a data collection plan so the problem behavior can be recorded, along with the setting events, antecedents, and consequences. The data gathered is quantitative and cannot infer causal relationships. It can, however, identify correlations between the different variables that will help us understand what is going on.

Collecting data is an important function and we need to put some thought into what data is needed and how it should be broken down. Data has key characteristics, and it is important to collect it in a way that it can be useful. For this, we stratify the data, i.e. we divide it into groups that will help explain the problem. For example, say we want a client to collect data on a dog charging a front door. If we collect data around the when, the where, what specific time, and who is present, we will have gathered much more information than if we were to focus only on the when and the how often.

In many situations we may make clients responsible for collecting any necessary data to help us determine what is going on. For example, we may ask them to record specific details about the problematic behavior for us to review. To assist clients, it is important to provide them with a data collection plan. This should include a form that identifies the stratification areas of data to be mined, and operational definitions that accurately define what the behavior is and what constitutes "a recordable event." (O'Heare, 2007, p. 196).

Important: Data Stratification

When we collect data it is important to collect stratification information too. This means determining which stratification labels are most important, such as "when," "what," "who" and "where." Stratifying data simply means that the data collected is placed into subcategories or groups to make it easier to use and analyze.

Remember, other than using pharmacological intervention to change a pet's brain chemistry, and thus his behavior, the only other way to change behavior is to alter, control or manipulate something in the pet's environment. We cannot magically impact behavior by focusing only on the B in the A-B-C contingency, we need to impact the antecedents, consequences or both.

Important questions to ask regarding your data collection plan:

- What are we trying to learn, track or evaluate?
- What will we count, and what will the measure be?
- How will the measure be collected? (E.g. duration, time, distance, latency, frequency, units).
- Does the data already exist or will new data be collected?
- Have we developed a data collection form for the client?
- Have we provided some simple operational definitions?
- Have we reviewed the data collection with the client to be sure they understand what they are collecting and how?
- Is the data collection plan necessary as a success factor?
- How long will data be collected for?

In data collection, your output variable Y is a function of X.

The Approach

A	Behavior	C
X variable	Y	X variable
Antecedent Measures	Behavior is a function of stimuli, i.e. antecedents or consequences	Consequence Measures

A good data collection plan also clarifies which dimensions of the behavior we would like the client to measure. A measurement planning worksheet can be helpful here (*see Figure 1-4*). It is not always necessary to measure every dimension. Rather, we should focus on the dimension that is most useful, given the behavior and its setting events.

For example, if a dog's barking is the main problem, we may determine that we only want the occurrences of barking recorded on the data collection plan. This would refer to the frequency dimension rather than the duration, i.e. how long the barking lasts. Before we can select which dimension we will measure, we will need to agree a goal statement with the client. If a client says they do not mind the dog barking each time somebody walks past the front door but that they want him to stop when they ask him to be quiet, then tracking the duration of the behavior may be more important than how often the dog barks.

Let us look at another example. When a puppy or adult dog is having problems with house soiling, the duration of the behavior is probably not important, but the frequency certainly is. Tracking data around duration or intensity will not help us understand when and why the dog soils the house. Instead, tracking frequency such as when, where, and who will be much more useful.

> **Important: Changing Behavior – The Y**
>
> *Remember that behavior is considered a dependent variable. We cannot change behavior unless we control or manipulate something in the environment. We can manipulate either the antecedent or the postcedent, i.e. the consequence.*

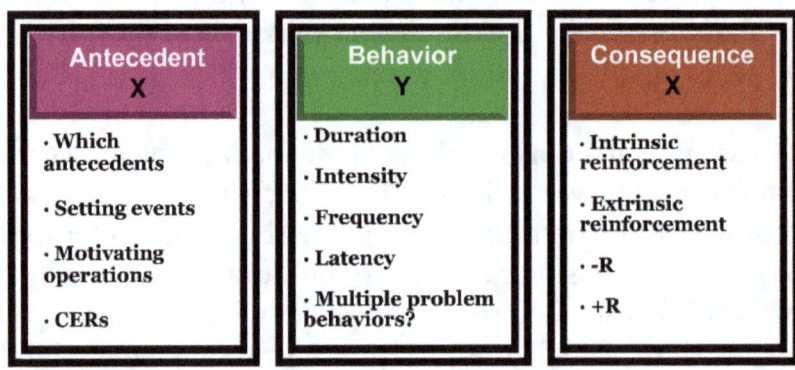

Figure 1-4: Potential Key Output Measures

When collecting data, it is best to obtain it from as few trials as possible without limiting its quality and accuracy. We need enough data to reveal patterns in the behavior so we can establish the trends. Meanwhile, we will need to decide who is going to collect the data. This person must be schooled in the correct process and must understand the necessity of remaining non-intrusive to ensure the data collection is stable, precise and unbiased. This means the collector should not in any way interfere with the behavior while recording the data in order to avoid a possible reduction in the informative value of the process.

It also means that if, for example, a client is measuring how

The Approach

often and for how long their dog barks at the front door, they should not react to the behavior any differently than if they were not recording the data points. *Note: If the problematic behavior is dangerous, we should actively attempt to prevent its occurrence through management and antecedent control procedures, and not encourage clients to measure it.*

Important: Measurement of Data

The goal of the measurement stage is to pinpoint the source of problems as precisely as we can by identifying process conditions and problems. The more precise we can be in our data collection, the easier it will be to analyze what is going on, when it is happening and how it is being reinforced. (Pande et al., 2002).

Operational Definitions

Writing operational definitions for data collection plans ensures all persons collect data in the same way.

Again, if the problem behavior is dangerous or poses a safety risk, then, as consultants, we must use our best professional judgment as to whether direct observation should be carried out or if strict and diligent management protocols need to be put into place.

At the end of the direct observation stage, it will be essential to revise the contingency statement developed during and after the informant interview. The data collection process will reveal new information about the functional relationship between all the variables, and may shed greater light on the problem.

The Functional Analysis

A functional analysis should only be carried out if the informant interview and direct observation have not revealed trends in the problem behavior, and/or components of the contingency statement are still unclear to the consultant.

Think about it like this: we cannot countercondition what we do not understand. This means that, if we cannot isolate the problematic antecedent, we cannot countercondition it, making behavior and emotional change very difficult. In addition, if we do not know what is reinforcing the behavior, we cannot control and manipulate environmental conditions to withhold reinforcement while we target another, more appropriate, behavior for reinforcement.

The functional analysis stage is a single subject experiment that tests the consultant's hypothesis, i.e. the contingency statement. The two most common single subject experiments used to analyze behavior are the reversal design and the alternating treatment design. The suitability of each experiment is determined by the hypothesis being tested. The functional analysis is designed to test the relationship between the hypothesized controlling antecedents and the behavior, and/or the hypothesized maintaining relationship between the behavior and its consequence.

Important: Single Subject Experiments

    a. *Reversal Design – The reversal design first establishes a baseline measure of the behavior. Either the antecedent or consequence is then presented and its impact on the behavior is measured as the behavior continues.*

    b. *Alternating Treatment Design – This design experiments with a reinforcing outcome and a punishment or extinction outcome to test for the contingency of consequences. There are clearly ethical considerations with an alternating treatment design as punishment contingencies are known to elicit fallout behaviors.*

Example of Antecedent-Behavior-Consequence

Antecedent: Traffic light turns red.

Behavior: Press foot onto brake.

Consequence: Stop at intersection.

The functional analysis sets up different independent variables and confirms or refutes their effect on the dependent variable, the behavior. The goal is to analyze what is, and what is not, evoking and/or maintaining the behavior so an effective behavior change program can be designed.

The single subject experiment should only cover areas of the contingency statement that are unclear. The consultant must also take into consideration that setting events and motivating operations should not be overlooked as they can contribute "indirectly to the contingencies." (O'Heare, 2007, p. 212).

Let us look at another example. We may feel very strongly that we can identify the antecedent eliciting the problematic behavior. However, we may be confused or unsure about how the problematic behavior is being reinforced. In this situation we would functionally analyze the postcedents only, i.e. everything that comes after the behavior. By doing this, we should be able to determine which postcedent is functionally related and thus the direct consequence maintaining the behavior.

In many of our behavior cases where we are dealing with operant behavior motivated through fear, i.e. a problematic conditioned emotional response, the priority will be to determine the specific and precise conditioned stimulus that elicits the conditioned response so we can develop an effective counterconditioning program (*see Figure 1-5*).

Figure 1-5: Example of Multiple Antecedents without a Clear Indication as to Which One Is Eliciting or Evoking the Problematic Behavior

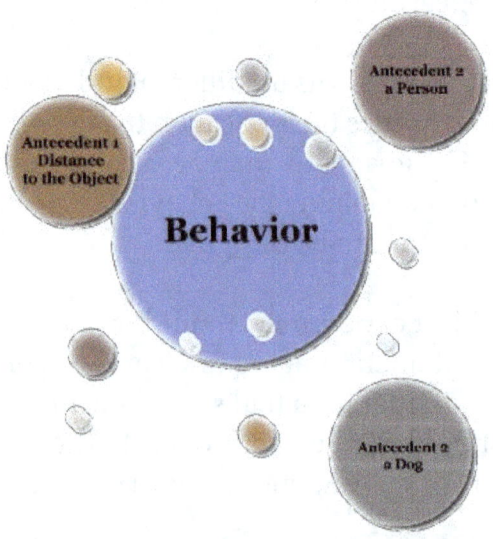

When conducting a functional analysis, the benefit and precision of the analysis must be weighed against the effort, time, skill required, and potential fallout of behavior rehearsing. A functional analysis should only be performed by a trained professional using a minimally invasive approach, a clearly defined plan to test only what is necessary, and a tangible goal. This must all be carefully considered with regard to the safety and security of all involved.

The Approach

The functional analysis should only be carried out if the important variables can be controlled throughout the experiment. Otherwise, the experiment will be flawed. Full informed consent must, of course, be obtained from the pet owner before this type of intervention is considered.

While functional analyses are a professional standard, there are considerations that have to be taken into account before conducting one. For example, it may be unethical to functionally analyze a behavior using the functional analysis method where deliberate manipulations are made that effectively encourage the pet to engage in the target behavior (O'Neill et al., 1997).

If a functional analysis is conducted, then it will be the third and final attempt to understand the behavior. As previously mentioned, a functional analysis should only be carried out after the unsuccessful use of an informant interview and direct observation, and if it is safe to do so. By now, we should have a very clear account of exactly what is happening, in what context, and how the problematic behavior is being reinforced. Together this forms a reliable contingency statement from which to develop a behavior change plan.

Example of a Complete Contingency Statement

<u>Distant Antecedents:</u>

The dog is on a walk with his female owner.

<u>Antecedent:</u>

A man with hat approaches directly from 18 feet away.

<u>Behavior:</u>

Barking, growling and lunging.

<u>Consequence:</u>

The man backs off (negative reinforcement).

<u>Prediction:</u>

The behavior will continue because it is being negatively reinforced, i.e. the dog's behavior is removing an aversive stimulus.

Having completed our functional assessment, we are now in an excellent position to develop our behavior change program.

Using Logic and Critical Thinking

Critical thinking and logic are extensive topics that fall much wider than the scope of this book. However, a lot of data is gathered during the functional assessment. How that data is used is important to ensure we make the best decisions for our clients and their pets. Using logic and critical thinking will help us better analyze and evaluate information so we can garnish the most knowledge from it. Critical thinking will engender a more rational and disciplined thinker as well as reduce prejudice and bias, providing us with a better understanding of our environment. Many of us have breed bias, or people bias, and this can affect or negatively impact how we approach and manage cases.

Critical thinking relates to how we make decisions and use our judgment. It is much more than simply how, or why, we think about things. It also incorporates how we take action from our thoughts, and how well we reason and remain open-minded. Deductive reasoning happens when we use our knowledge of one thing, process or statement to determine if another thing, process or statement is true. Our reasoning does not always follow logic as it can often be controlled by our emotions and our biases. Reasoning is described as "drawing conclusions on the basis of reasons." (Paul, 2008, p. 20).

The study of logic is a branch of philosophy that provides the rules for deriving valid conclusions. The concept of logical form is central to logic, and it is held that the validity of an argument is determined by its logical form, not by its content. "Logic refers simply to the principles that apply to the assessment of that process." (Paul, 2008, p. 20).

Any conclusions we draw are only valid if the conclusion is derived from accepted facts. For example, we know that $100 \div 5 = 20$. There is a mathematical rule or premise that determines how this is calculated and we consider it logical. If I said that $4 \times 3 \times 1 = 234$ we would all agree that this is illogical, no matter how I try to explain my answer.

To engage in critical thinking, we must keep an open mind. This can be difficult when faced with emotionally charged situations but being open minded is how we learn. By considering new evidence or arguments we can challenge how we currently think or feel about an issue. It is essential to be able to consider other possibilities rather than remain entrenched in our own preconceived notions.

In the same way, we should ensure we do not allow our predetermined opinions to influence the way we evaluate data to the degree that we use it to confirm what we already believe. Instead we must remain open minded with our clients and be receptive to their ideas and opinions. Even though clients do not have the skills and knowledge professionals bring to the table their input can often be very valuable in achieving their goals for their pet's behavior.

Keeping a keen sense of objectivity will also help oppose any natural biases we may have and help us evaluate information more thoroughly.

> **Important: The Voice of the Customer**
>
> *The voice of the customer is the term used to describe the stated and unstated needs or requirements of our customers. It is captured during the informant interview, and is then updated if necessary as the behavior change program evolves. Six Sigma is a disciplined, data-driven approach and methodology for project management.*

Establishing the Voice of the Customer

To help clients make improvements regarding their pets' behavior and training goals, it is important that we determine what is important to the people affected by the process.

The client is not just the person who contacts us and sets up the appointment, but anyone who will be impacted by the program and its goals. This means we must take into consideration all the stakeholders who will be affected by the process and the outcome. It includes family members, in-home service providers, grandparents, friends and other visitors to the home. We need to obtain their collective voice and ascertain what is important to them. These form the critical to quality components (CTQ), which are then translated into specifications. These

The Approach

specifications are objective and have measurable criteria. They will define the goal and what success will look like when the program is complete (*see Figure 1-6*).

To develop CTQ specifications we have to really understand what clients want and hope to achieve and be smart about the way we question them. Through the question and answer process we can then develop our program goals and ensure that they meet the needs of all involved. For example, the CTQs of the parents and grandparents may be different yet equally as important to the outcome or the future of the pet.

Figure 1-6: Translating the Voice of the Customer

Customer Comment	Image or Issue	CTQ Requirement
What we hear from our clients	What need/issue does this represent to the customer?	What specific requirement or action addresses the issue?
"My dog jumps on the children"	A safety issue	The dog must keep all four paws on the ground unless cued to jump

The voice of the customer will help drive and determine our data collection plan. Think about it this way: What does success look like to the client? Can the client describe in tangible terms their exact expectations of the training program? If this can be done, we have a measurement goal that everyone understands as well as shared meaning. We are all on the same page about where we are headed and what success will look like. This will be our goal post, and when we reach it we will know we have achieved what we set out to do.

Figure 1-6 cites some examples of CTQ requirements. The

client has stated that the dog jumps on the children and this is a safety issue for the family. The tangible CTQ for the client involves the dog keeping four feet on the ground. For professionals, this means the dog does not jump unless cued to jump. When a client tells us the problem is the dog jumping on people and they want him to stop it is not a goal. What specifically do they want? What is critical for them? Do they want the dog to sit? Do they want him to just keep four feet on the ground? Do they want him to lie down? What exactly are they looking for? It needs to be very specific. When this has been established, we have created shared meaning. We have a plan and we can begin.

Having defined this CTQ requirement, everyone involved in the program will now understand what success will look like. We have identified the various customers who will be involved in the process, asked them what the issues are, and, finally, translated these specific issues or problems into measurable requirements.

Figure 1-7 depicts a form that helps pulls all the deliverables from a functional assessment together. This includes an analysis of the A-B-C contingency, a hypothesis of what is going on with the current problematic behavior, and the necessary CTQs to help reach the client's goals.

The Approach

	Figure 1-7: Functional Assessment Deliverables	
Antecedents What happens immediately before the behavior?	**Behavior** What is the behavior?	**Consequence** What happens immediately after the behavior?
1. What are the setting events? See page 14. 2. What are the motivating operations? See page 14. 3. Can you identify the conditioned stimulus (CS) that is eliciting the reflexive behavior? Or: 4. The discriminative stimulus (S^D) for operant behaviors.	Operant Behavior (observable and measurable) • Duration. • Frequency. • Intensity. • Latency. • Behavior topography.	1. How is the behavior currently being reinforced? +R or −R? 2. Is punishment taking place? If so, in what form? This will be impacting the conditioned emotional response (CER), which is a motivating operation for the operant behavior being observed.
Hypothesis – A reliable contingency statement.			

Antecedent	Behavior	Consequence	Prediction

copyright Niki Tudge 2017

Client Comment – What we hear from our clients.	Issue – The precise problem: What need or issue does this represent to our client?	Critical to Quality Measure (CTQ): What specific requirement or action addresses this issue?
• The dog is a pain, he jumps on visitors as they arrive!	• This is embarrassing for us and physically dangerous for our elderly parents and young visitors when they enter our home.	• The dog will sit politely for front door entrances and greetings.
• My dog is difficult to walk on a leash so we no longer go out every day.	• It is embarrassing and uncomfortable to walk my dog who pulls and lunges all the time.	• I want to be able to walk my dog each evening for 30 minutes without the constant tugging and lunging at other dogs and people.

The Planning

We now move into the planning phase of our training program. In order to function successfully as consultants and trainers, we need to plan and control every step. Planning comprises a series of activities, which have a start and end point geared towards accomplishing a set goal using the resources available. Planning is a management process and we have a joint responsibility with our clients to attain our goals (Mullins, 2002).

According to Kerzner (2001, p. 550), planning is "decision making based on futurity." In other words, it is a continuous process of making decisions, which we must do actively when working on behavior change programs. The process is often fluid and the plan may need to be tweaked and changed but this is preferable to stumbling along without any plan at all. Without proper planning, we will not meet our timeline or achieve our goals and this can disappoint and frustrate clients.

Most planning elements, such as actions, resources, time management and goal implementation are equally as important, whether we are training just one individual or a group, and can be applied across the different services in our businesses. When we begin to put together our project plan we must consider how the training plan will look, where we will start and at what skill level. Will we be implementing a complete behavior change program or is the client interested in a management plan only? What is the client's current baseline measurement in terms of the skills they have already mastered? Who are the stakeholders, i.e. who else has a vested interest in this behavior change or training program and needs to be involved in the plan?

The Training/Behavior Change Program

The purpose of conducting training sessions is to deliver results for our clients and their pets. We embark on training because we believe it will help our clients and in some way improve their pet management, care and training performance and thus improve the behavior of their pets.

Personally, during the initial informant interview stage, I am already considering the many options that are available and relevant to the client's situation. I need to be able to answer the following questions with confidence so I can formulate the best plan possible:

- Where is the client now on the mastery scale of training skills? In other words, what do they know and what can they already do to a high level of competency?

- How big is the skill gap between the pet's current behavior and the goal statement agreed with the client?

- What is the family's lifestyle and how active are individual family members? What do each of them contribute?

The Planning

- How many family members are invested in the daily care of the pet and the pet's future training?

- What do we believe their level of commitment to be in terms of both the financial and time investments?

- How compliant do we feel the clients will be even though we have discussed and agreed on the psychological contract?

None of my individual thoughts or self-drawn answers are judgments. They are merely realistic criteria to consider when I am tentatively devising my personalized training program for the family and what I believe is best for them in their current situation with the constraints and challenges we may face.

How Will the Plan Look?

Some of the key points that must be considered to determine how the training plan might look include:

1. Is there a difference between how the pet behaves and interacts with different family members?

2. Is there a real opportunity for improvement? We like to think, especially as trainers, that there are many ways we can help improve a dog's behavior. We must remember, however, the client's goals and adhere to protocols that will reach these goals in the most expedient way.

3. We need to establish who in the family will be involved in the training process and who *should* be participating in the training process. If a family member is very instrumental in the care of the pet, they must be encouraged to take part in the training sessions.

4. Are there the necessary systems in place to support the training we are about to begin? For example:

   a. What changes need to be made to the dog's living environment?

   b. What changes need to be adopted by the family members?

   c. What equipment will need to be purchased to support the training program?

   d. How much time needs to be allocated to management, exercise, feeding, training, and care?

   e. Will the pet's behavior be improved via a basic obedience program or a full-on behavior change program?

Key Question

Will the pet's behavior be improved via the implementation of management tactics? Will he need a basic obedience training program, or does he require a full-on behavior change program?

Point "e" above is very significant. In my opinion, there are noteworthy differences between a dog trainer and a dog behavior consultant as well as the roles they play and their individual skill sets.

Pet dog training helps clients teach their dog new skills that will help him better coexist in our human world. Professional trainers help their clients build obedience behavior repertoires, which may involve teaching a dog new skills, such as a "sit/stay" to prevent him from begging at the table, or teaching him to "come" when the owner wants him to return.

The Planning

Behavior counseling, on the other hand, requires the involvement of a qualified behavior consultant who works with a client to help change an existing problematic behavior. Many behavior problems present with an element of fear as their emotional foundation, which is often manifested as anxiety, anger or frustration. Fear is a very normal "self-protective" response for dogs as, in order to survive, they have to be good at adapting and reacting to potentially dangerous situations.

Fear in dogs is either innate, which means it has an evolutionary significance (such as a fear of loud noises, strangers, isolation or fire) or is ontogenic, which means it has been learned through experience. Changing a problematic behavior or a conditioned emotional response requires a broad understanding of learning and behavior, combined with a toolbox of specialized skills to implement the appropriate behavior change protocol. It is not possible to train fear out of a dog or resolve aggression simply by teaching a dog obedience skills.

To demonstrate the difference between the two courses of action, I will detail a behavior modification protocol based on helping a dog with separation distress and then compare it with the basic common training issue of how to teach a dog to sit. This comparison will show the complexity of handling a behavior change program versus the teaching of a new skill to a well-rounded dog.

First though, we will examine how respondent conditioning works and how our knowledge of this can help us to resolve complicated behavior cases as a result of problematic conditioned emotional responses. In the early 20th century, Russian physiologist Ivan Pavlov was engaged in some award-winning work on the digestive system, and was studying the role of saliva in dogs. While he was conducting his experiments, he stumbled upon something he referred to as "psychic reflexes."

Within an organism there are two types of reflexes: unconditioned and conditioned. An unconditioned reflex (UR) is unlearned and occurs unconditionally, whereas a conditioned reflex (CR) is acquired and considered impermanent.

An unconditioned reflex consists of an unconditioned stimulus (US) and an unconditioned response (UR). An unconditioned stimulus is something that, when presented, evokes a natural, unconditioned, response. Examples would be blinking when air is blown towards the eyelid, or sweating when stressed or scared. Unconditioned reflexes are important for an animal's survival. Freeze-dried liver offered to a dog is an example of a US, and the dog drooling as a result is an example of the resulting UR.

A conditioned reflex occurs when a conditioned stimulus (CS) creates a conditioned response (CR). This is a learned response to a given set of conditions occurring in the environment. Pavlov recognized that any stimulus could become a conditioned stimulus when paired repeatedly with an unconditioned stimulus (Chance 2008 p 64).

In 1924, American psychologist Mary Cover Jones recognized that, if a CS for fear is paired with a positive US, then the conditioned emotional response (CER) could be modified. This used respondent conditioning to reverse the unwanted effects of previous conditioning, and is known as counterconditioning (*see page 39*). Because the pet is gradually exposed to the fearful stimulus, this process has been called exposure therapy.

The Planning

Systematic desensitization is a more recent form of exposure therapy and involves the promotion of relaxation, as well as graded exposure to the fearful stimulus paired with counter conditioning.

> *Important: What Is Systematic Desensitization?*
>
> *Systematic desensitization is a graded exposure through a hierarchy of stimulus intensity where, at each level, it is suggested that respondent extinction or counterconditioning is taking place.*
>
> *There are three components to systematic desensitization:*
>
> - ✓ *Hierarchy of stimulus intensity.*
> - ✓ *Graded exposure through the hierarchy.*
> - ✓ *Counterconditioning throughout.*

Systematic Desensitization and Counterconditioning

If a dog is showing signs of fear or panic, then the antecedent is having an aversive effect and the behavior is being negatively reinforced. Behavior change programs for dogs presenting with such behaviors must be based on protocols associated with respondent conditioning.

Prior to developing a systematic desensitization protocol we must first complete a functional assessment and have a contingency statement we are extremely confident about. The contingency statement must identify controlling antecedents and the behavior, and/or the hypothesized maintaining relationship between the behavior and its consequence. A determination can then be made about which behavior change protocols should be used: respondent, operant or a combination of both. Systematic desensitization protocols are used to change behaviors that are controlled by the autonomic nervous system, which are driven by emotions such as fear, panic and anxiety. The goal is to change the respondent(s), i.e. the conditioned emotional response(s).

To effectively design a systematic desensitization protocol, we need to know the specific conditioned stimulus that elicits the fear, panic or anxiety so we can construct a graded hierarchy starting with levels that only elicit attention, as opposed to sensitization, or potentiation.

When planning the graded hierarchy we need to take into consideration the stimulus variables that could elicit emotional responses, such as distance, duration of exposure, distractions in the environment, orientation of the stimulus, and any motion or contrast within the stimulus exposure. For each of these variables we will need to develop a stimulus exposure hierarchy.

When designing the systematic desensitization plan we also need to have knowledge of the setting events that provide the context for and influence the behavior. It is important to recognize that respondent behaviors motivate operants because they establish operations, making it "more likely" that the animal will engage in "escape or avoidance behavior." (Miltenberger, 2004).

The Planning

> ***Important: What Is Sensitization and Habituation?***
>
> *Reflexes are the relationship between a specific event and specific response. By nature, reflexes are stereotypic, but the strength of a reflex response can be altered. When there is a reduction in response to a specific stimulus after repeated exposures to it, it is known as habituation. Sensitization occurs when repeated exposure or a single exposure to a stimulus increases the intensity of the response. Habituation and sensitization are considered non-associative learning.*

Understanding if the operants are being negatively or positively reinforced is important. As already explained, if the antecedent is aversive, then the behavior is being negatively reinforced. If we can provide the same reinforcement for a more suitable behavior, then the process of generalization can be expedited and behavior maintenance may be more easily supported in the future.

When constructing a systematic desensitization protocol, it is critical to ensure the pet begins the process in a relaxed, happy manner and stays this way throughout each of the trials, i.e. at sub-threshold. Otherwise counterconditioning cannot occur. A positive emotional state is incompatible with anxiety or fear. Too many desensitization and counterconditioning programs begin with a pet that is "neutral," which is counterproductive to our goals.

Too much excitement (i.e. if the animal is too distracted from the problem stimulus) can also negatively impact the counterconditioning process. The idea is to positively reinforce calm, operant behaviors to encourage and maintain a happy and relaxed state.

During the counterconditioning component of the systematic desensitization process there must be a contrast between the "open bar" and the "closed bar." In other words, when the fear eliciting stimulus is presented, all great things happen. These are then quickly removed with the exit of the fear eliciting stimulus. There must be both a temporal relationship and a contingency between the conditioned stimulus and the unconditioned stimulus for conditioning to occur and for the problematic emotional response to be replaced with a new, more appropriate response (O'Heare, 2009).

It is more effective during counterconditioning to have fewer trials but that each one be successful, rather than rush the process and set ourselves (and the dog) up for failure.

Important: What Is Generalization?

When an animal has learned a behavior in one situation and the behavior carries over to a different situation, then the behavior is said to have generalized. (Chance, 2008 p. 301).

A Sample Outline of a Behavior Change Case - Separation Anxiety

Evidence shows that separation distress-related behaviors are respondent behaviors, a combination of the body's panic and fear systems. The amygdala, a section of the brain that stores memories associated with emotional events, activates behavioral and emotional responses to fear (Lindsay, 2005). Because of memories that elicit a problematic conditioned response, pets can perform operant behaviors that are destructive to both themselves and their environment.

Separation distress is defined as "physical or behavioral signs of distress or panic… only in the absence of, or lack of access to, the attachment object." (O'Heare, 2004, p. 31). To change this emotional state, an individual behavior change program must be developed and based on a functional assessment.

To start with, we should rule out any existing medical conditions that may be causing problematic behaviors. We also need to eliminate the possibility that some behaviors manifest themselves as separation distress but are actually based on other inadequacies in the dog's life, such as boredom, lack of exercise, external distractions or inadequate mental stimulation. Problematic behaviors that may result in such cases include excessive barking, whining, chewing and other displacement behaviors.

The extent of our behavior change program will be based on the severity of the problem, the owner's goals and level of commitment. In some minor cases it may only be necessary to implement daily management protocols to keep everyone relaxed, safe and sound. More severe cases will require daily management, counterconditioning and a systematic desensitization program.

As with any type of behavior modification program, punishment and any form of harsh treatment should be avoided at all costs. A dog that exhibits separation distress behaviors has lost his ability to form healthy relationships with the "object of attachment." He is not able to predict or control his basic need for safety, and has no ability to "establish an adaptive behavioral framework." (Lindsay, 2005, p. 198). His environment must become predictable and stable so he can begin to establish a healthy relationship with the attachment object (O'Heare, 2004).

Important: What Is Shaping?

Reinforcing small approximations of a desired behavior in succession to achieve a more complicated behavior is called shaping. Behavior shaping can be used to achieve complicated behaviors that do not occur naturally or, as a behavior analyst would say, they are not in the learner's current repertoire. They are behaviors that cannot be captured, or are too complicated to lure. (Chance, 2008).

Research shows that punitive rearing practices, traumatic experiences, isolation and rehoming can be considered risk factors to separation distress behaviors.

As a foundation, the dog in question should undergo basic obedience training using the least invasive methods. Shaping is the preferred tool for developing operant behaviors as it empowers the dog to experiment with alternative behaviors, helping him grow in confidence while developing social independence.

Daily training exercises also engage the dog in pleasurable activities that provide mental stimulation as they restrict the limbic system from activating negative emotional responses (O'Heare, 2005). Obedience training also heightens a dog's "attentional and impulse control abilities two vital cortical executive functions" that are supportive of his ability to adapt under stress (Lindsay, 2005, p. 226). Newly acquired obedience behaviors can be incorporated into everyday situations and the dog should then only have access to highly valued resources through the owner. This encourages him to look to his owner for guidance. Through positive reinforcement protocols the dog will become more empowered and feel more confident to make the right choices from environmental and owner-led cues.

A more specialized and pertinent diet may be helpful for dogs that experience high levels of stress. Foods that contain wheat, corn, animal by-products, chemicals and/or inadequate protein levels can significantly impact behavior. Diets deficient in certain amino acids can impact the serotonin levels in a dog's brain, causing him to be more emotional, overly reactive and sensitive. Always refer clients to a veterinarian or canine nutritionist for dietary advice and recommendations.

A very structured, fun exercise schedule must be put in place for a dog exhibiting separation distress behaviors as exercise plays an important role in managing stress. It has a therapeutic effect on a dog's physiological state in that it induces the release of endorphins and enhances serotonin activity. This supports the regulation of mood and the control of impulsive behaviors (Lindsay, 2000). A dog that is appropriately exercised will be more relaxed, contributing to a healthier state of mind. It will also assist with any obedience training exercises because the dog has been set up to be able to learn new things.

In contrast to a case such as this, I will now briefly detail a basic training protocol for teaching a dog to sit on cue.

A Sample Outline of a Training Situation – Teaching a Dog to Sit

Teaching a dog to "sit" can be done by capturing, targeting or luring. These are behavior acquisition methods and there are pros and cons to each. The important factor is that the learning environment is safe, fun and includes lots of positive reinforcement. I always feel it is necessary to point out to clients that we do not actually teach a dog to sit. Dogs can already do this from a very early age. We do not teach them to lie down or come back either. These are, in fact, all natural behaviors. All we do is put them under stimulus control. In other words, we train a dog to be motivated enough to engage in whatever behavior we request because it brings him something of value, such as a cookie, attention or a toy (*see Figure 2-1*).

Figure 2-1: The Three-Term Contingency

Antecedent - Behavior - Consequence

The "Sit" Cue   The "Sit" Behavior   The "Sit" Reinforcement +R

But back to teaching a sit. Whether the sit behavior is lured or captured, the behavior is marked and reinforcement delivered as soon as the dog's rump hits the floor. For many of us, this means clicking and treating, or saying "yes," then delivering the treat. The dog is reinforced for a one-second sit and we repeat this five times. Between each trial the dog is encouraged to move forward as the handler moves backwards calling his name. This resets the dog so the next trial can be performed. Alternatively, a reset cookie can be used. Simply toss the cookie away from the dog and, when he has eaten it, he returns for another trial.

The sit behavior is then built into a short duration behavior by reinforcing it after three seconds and then five seconds in sets of five. When the dog will sit reliably for five seconds (and if the behavior has been captured as opposed to lured), we then introduce the hand signal and/or the verbal cue, "sit." This means the next time the dog begins to sit we immediately give the hand signal. If the behavior has been lured, this is when we begin to fade food from the hand motion.

When the dog is reliably sitting for five seconds from either a hand signal or the verbal cue, we then switch to an intermittent reinforcement schedule. At this juncture, we will decide if we are going to build on the sit behavior for duration or distance, and will work on only one dimension at a time until the end behavior is achieved. When new dimensions are introduced, reinforcement will return to a more frequent schedule until the dog has mastered the raised criteria (*see Figure 2-2*).

When we are first teaching a new behavior it is important to use continuous reinforcement. This means the behavior is reinforced each time it occurs, i.e. a schedule of one reinforcer for one response. Because each operant is reinforced the increase in the rate of behavior is rapid. However, continuous reinforcement offers little resistance to extinction and produces stereotyped response topography, i.e. responses are relatively invariant over successive occurrences.

Continuous reinforcement is rare in a natural environment where most behavior is reinforced on an intermittent schedule. In intermittent schedules of reinforcement, only some, not all, behavioral responses are reinforced. Intermittent schedules include ratio schedules of reinforcement and interval schedules of reinforcement. Ratio schedules are based on a set number of responses given prior to reinforcement, while interval schedules operate on a set amount of time passing prior to reinforcement delivery. Both ratio and interval schedules can work on a fixed or a variable, random schedule of reinforcement (Pierce and Cheney, 2004).

Important: What Is Extinction?

Operant extinction is when the consequences that reinforced a behavior are withheld and the strength of the behavior is weakened. Initially, the effect of withholding the consequence that previously reinforced a behavior may abruptly increase the behavior. This is referred to as extinction burst. The previously reinforced behavior may also become more variable in an attempt to elicit reinforcement. Operant extinction can increase the frequency of emotional behaviors such as aggression. (Chance, 2008, p. 158).

Figure 2-2: The Different Reinforcement Schedules Used over Number of Responses and Minutes

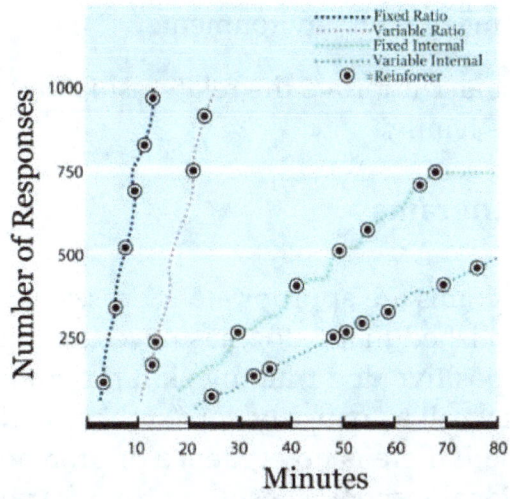

Behavior Change, Training or Management?

In my professional capacity, I advise toward considering three possible singular approaches, or a combination of two or more.

Management Only

Management refers to situations when clients do not wish to undergo full behavior change programs for whatever reason. In such cases, it becomes our role to best advise them on the most appropriate management activities. This aims to:

a. Reduce the likelihood of the problematic behavior occurring by changing the pet's environment and controlling the problematic stimulus.

b. Facilitate better education so the client understands canine behavior and social communication.

c. Ensure the most appropriate equipment is being used for the welfare of all concerned, e.g. crates, leashes, treats, etc.

d. Provide the pet with the necessary mental and physical enrichment in his environment.

e. Impact and improve the relationship between the pet and his family.

Training Programs

Training programs are appropriate for cases where we have quickly established that a dog has never had the benefit of attending a positive dog training skill program, or is what the client may call a "naughty" or "stubborn" dog. In cases like this, where there is no evidence of problematic conditioned emotional responses resulting from fear-based issues, we simply need to help the owner teach the pet how to live happily amongst humans.

These types of programs will include some management activities in the form of antecedent control to prevent inappropriate behavior occurring while we train the dog new skills. We will progress very quickly in terms of getting the job done and teaching the necessary behaviors, such as sit, down, come, stay, off, leave, okay, relax, go to your crate, on your mat etc. More often than not the program will commence as soon as the informant interview is complete. Often in the first session we are already talking to our clients about "charging the clicker," and how to capture, target and lure new behaviors. By the end of this session we will be comfortably leaving our clients with some homework to complete, while they feel happy they can impact their pet's behavior positively through a fun process.

The Planning

Behavior Change Programs

Behavior change programs are far more complicated and require a different set of practitioner skills, as well as a more in-depth knowledge of consulting skills. They require a competent understanding of learning and behavior, canine communication and social behavior, and respondent conditioning protocols and procedures. These types of programs will enlist activities from the previous section on management (*see page 49*) but will also utilize the empowering effect of teaching a dog new skills via positive reinforcement and negative punishment. In addition, they will involve the implementation of full systematic desensitization and counterconditioning program, as detailed on page 39-40.

Active and ongoing project management is a key component in working through a behavior change case, and the following will all need to be incorporated into the plan:

1. Gathering of all the pertinent information – The Approach.

2. Understanding the problematic stimulus so a counterconditioning program will be effective – The Approach.

3. Understanding of current reinforcement - The Approach.

4. Prevention of problematic behaviors – Management Activities.

5. Teaching new skills – Training Program.

6. Systematic desensitization and counterconditioning sessions – Behavior Change Activities.

7. Lesson planning and order of events – Training Plan.

It is easy to see and understand why, when we communicate

these options to our clients, they do not want, or cannot commit to a full behavior change program. For a start it will be far more time intensive, and because most behavior change programs have to be conducted as private sessions, it can place them out of reach financially for many clients.

If we plan appropriately during this initial stage, then we will know whether we are starting a short session (or sessions) for management activity implementation, training skill sessions to teach the pet new skills, or a full behavior change program. We will then be able to schedule our lesson plans, content, order of activities and potential outcomes. Without an appropriate plan, results may be inconsistent and less effective.

Skill Gap Analysis - Baseline Measurements

During the functional assessment, we will have taken baseline measurements of the pet's problematic behavior. At this stage we should also know what skills the pet has in his current repertoire and to what level of competence. This will enable us to define the appropriate starting point for any lesson planning. Clients do not appreciate it when we waste their time or duplicate efforts, so having baseline measures is really important. If a client informs us their dog can already do a sit/stay, then we can test the cue in different contexts. Rather than begin a program with an assumption about what sit/stay looks like, we need to create shared meaning with the client about their dog's actual performance level. This way we will begin where we need to, i.e. at the point of competence, and not before or after.

Baseline measures also help us to determine what we need to do next to reach our goal, which is to change the form of the behavior and/or its frequency, intensity, duration, latency, or rate. It is important to quantify the baseline behavior in terms

The Planning

of these criteria so an effective training objective can be set. Training sessions and behavior dimensions should be tracked so it is easy to assess, in a quantifiable manner, whether the process is working, or whether it needs to be evaluated and amended as we work towards our goal.

In terms of our clients, we need to understand and analyze the skill gap we have here too. For example:

- What do the clients know?
- What do they not know?
- Have they been involved in pet training before?
- What belief systems do they bring to the table?
- How flexible is their approach to our methods, philosophy and game plan?

One of the reasons many training programs do not yield the expected results is because they are launched without the relevant knowledge regarding gaps in the client's skills and knowledge. If there are philosophical differences, then these need to be addressed at the onset and not three lessons into the program.

The Environment

Learning and memory are closely related concepts. The former refers to the acquisition of skills or knowledge, while the latter is the expression of what has been acquired. The quality of the learning or training environment should not be overlooked for one critical reason: It must be conducive to students being able to store newly learned information so they can retrieve and use it later.

Creating Connections between Learning and Memory

A review of the literature from the 1940s suggests that there are two kinds of memories: those that know "what" and those that know "that." The memory systems of the brain work in parallel to support behavior, and memories are recalled or revealed when there is a reactivation of the systems within which the learning originally occurred.

For example, if someone was hurt by a dog as a child, it can create a stable declarative memory of the event, as well as a non-declarative fear of dogs. This fear may eventually become experienced as a personality trait rather than a memory. In other words, the person may be viewed as having a phobia about dogs (Squire, 2004).

When learning new skills, it often helps students remember if they do something active with the new information. Because working memory has a short duration and information passing through this part of the system has to be processed quickly, students have to be conscientious and decisive in how they interact and process the new knowledge or skill.

During the processing stage, students need to pass information through the feedback loop (*see Figure 3-1*). This means an instructor may ask them whether they can explain what they have learned, or test them on why they are doing what they are doing. Practice helps but it must focus on quality rather than quantity.

We have all heard of muscle memory. This does not actually refer to a memory that is stored in the muscles of the body in spite of the way it sounds. In reality, it refers to memories stored in the brain that are much like a collection of regular tasks, and the muscles required to engage in them. Muscle memory does not impact or judge whether a skill is being performed correctly. This is the role of the trainer or coach. Positive, informative coaching will help students develop the correct mechanics, i.e. muscle memory, before they are left on their own to practice and strengthen their learning.

Figure 3-1: The Feedback Loop

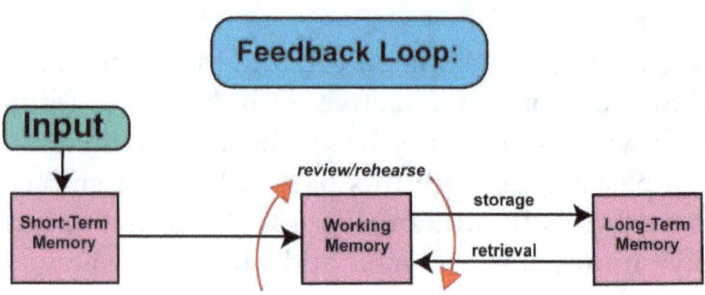

In order for learning and memory to be optimized, the experience has to be fun. This is one of the most controllable aspects of the training environment. Fun is incompatible with stress, which is detrimental to the learning process. According to Levy (2014), stress prevents memory storage because "learning and memory storage happens effectively when neurons are repeatedly activated across their synapses — a process that effectively tells the brain that a stimulus, behavior or habit is important to retain."

Environmental Pressure

Any training environment has the potential to exert pressure on students, and this can also manifest itself as stress. There are three key types of stress typically found in the training environment: unintended, intended and environmental.

Unintended stress can be defined as stress that is not purposely placed on the trainee. It comes about as the result of poor preparation on the part of the trainer and can hinder the learning process. If we think about a time when we might have started a training session then realized we did not have the necessary equipment, or simply forgot where we were in the overall plan, our failure to be fully prepared may well create diversions and floundering on our part and place unintended stress on our students.

Conversely, intended stress derives from the actual training conditions. It should be positive and increase students' interest levels to create an optimal learning environment. Positive stressors should create skill-based or intellectual challenges that help students grow. They should in no way become aversive, and students should not fear or attempt to avoid them. The timing of training scenarios, or decision making and problem solving opportunities, can be positive stressors that students will embrace if they have been set up to succeed and are ready for the challenge.

Important: What Is Trigger Stacking?

Trigger stacking takes place when a dog or person is exposed to a series of problematic stimuli over a short period of time. Any of the stimuli alone may not be enough to elicit a problematic response, but when stacked together, they compound the problem.

Lastly, there is the issue of environmental stress, which will naturally occur in the training environment. It is considered the "background or baseline conditions that may be part of a learning environment, but can still hinder the learning process." (Davis, 2009, p.5). For example, our training environment may provide excessive noise, have poor lighting, or use equipment that makes for an uncomfortable experience. Sometimes the trainer can be perceived as intimidating by students and this can be stressful too. As trainers, we must always be cognizant of trigger stacking and understand how these multiple sources of somewhat inconsequential stress, when compounded, can greatly impact students' ability to learn. Ultimately, they determine if the session is going to be productive and fun or not.

> *Like most jobs, the bulk of being a trainer is the consistent and regular application of basic skills and techniques that produce results… It's not the flair for dramatics or unorthodox styles that educate students, despite the movies that glamorise otherwise. These basic manoeuvres are the simple steps that must be repeated over and over again to complete the journey from complete novice to competent practitioner. (Davis, 2005).*

Any training environment should best reflect the real world. This means that it must, as far as is possible, replicate any location where students will need to successfully implement the training.

If we are working with a private client and one of their goals is to prevent their pet from entering the kitchen while they are preparing dinner, then the kitchen is where the training should take place. Training should progress up the skill criteria ladder with each step being more difficult than the last, but all should be within the context of where the behavior is expected to be performed.

An example might involve teaching a client to train their pet to "leave it." In this specific context, the client's goal is for the cue to apply when their five-year-old child drops food on the floor. The training environment needs to incorporate all the normal setting events that occur in real life.

Situations such as this are where I think group classes often fall flat in terms of meeting clients' goals. Encouraging clients

The Environment

to sign up for a set of classes to address a problem or a few problems that are not even in the class curriculum seems rather counterproductive to me. I believe we set ourselves up for failure in many situations because we try to squeeze clients into pre-existing service offerings that do not best provide solutions to their real life problems. Yes, one can argue that if a client learns "leave it" in a group, then it can be applied to real world scenarios in the home. However, I would question whether most clients leaving group classes receive that level of support and post-group class tuition or follow-up. It is difficult enough when working with group classes to make it through the actual curriculum, let alone help each individual transfer these rudimentary skills to real life scenarios. Furthermore, this makes the assumption that the group classes are effectively working through the learning cycle. In my experience, they are more likely to consist of a series of uncomfortable lecture sessions, often with everyone on their feet throughout, no climate control, and very little hands-on practice and supervision.

Coaching for Results

In my first book, *People Training Skills for Pet Professionals*, I covered nine skills I feel anyone who engages in professional training or coaching should be competent in. These nine skills are:

- Formalizing each person's role.
- Managing our clients through change.
- Managing our client's training performance.
- Managing and resolving conflict.
- Grasping and using the power of persuasion.
- Building client commitment and compliance.
- Employing the art of giving and receiving feedback.

- Managing client anger.
- Effective time management.

I will now list additional skills that I think are needed during the actual hands-on training process.

Motivation

Motivation can be described as the direction and persistence of action, or why people do what they do. It is an individual phenomenon and is usually intentional and multifaceted.

Motivation is the force that drives an individual to attempt to achieve a goal. As such, individual performance can be described as the combination of a person's ability and motivation. If students have ability but no motivation, they will not perform or exhibit the required behavior. Alternatively, if they are motivated but lack the necessary skills, it will restrict their performance. A student's level of motivation is also affected by their individual emotional state at any given time in any given context. Depending on whether their emotional state is positive or negative, it will either facilitate or inhibit motivation and, thus, learning.

If a student's motivation during a training session is blocked before reaching the desired goal, there are two possible outcomes. The first is the constructive approach, whereby the individual concerned tries out other avenues or behaviors to achieve the desired goal. The second is frustration, which can result in stress, anxiety, anger, or withdrawal from the session. Students that have a positive learning and reinforcement history are more likely to attempt a constructive behavior approach when their motivational drive is blocked rather than revert to anger or withdrawal.

The Environment

There are several factors that influence the level of frustration a student may experience during a training or coaching session, including their level of need, what they have invested in the process so far, and the degree of attachment they have to the goals. If a student's motivation is blocked, the level of frustration exhibited will also be dependent on the perceived nature of the blocking component, as well as the adaptability and resilience of the student.

As trainers, it is important that we structure our training sessions effectively to prevent high levels of frustration developing. We can do this by supplying ample amounts of reinforcement, communicating effectively with students, and encouraging their active participation. As professionals, we need to moderate the task difficulty and take personal responsibility to ensure students' skills are tested before moving to new and more difficult criteria. Professional trainers also give upbeat, clear and unambiguous feedback while ensuring the training session is innovative and adequately challenging, given students' skills and motivation.

Ultimately, motivation is the driving force within students by which they attempt to achieve their training goals in order to fulfill a specific need or expectation. To become effective and efficient people trainers, we need to recognize the importance of using appropriate reinforcement during the learning stage of each behavior. As such, we need to give clear direction and use effective, fair, motivating training procedures, and create training environments that facilitate a constructive approach over a frustrated approach.

Motivating students is a key part of coaching. In the work place we can incentivize employees and contractors with performance bonuses, but in our work, we cannot use money as a motivator as we do not pay our students or clients. Students deserve a positive training environment and a good relationship with their teacher in order to thrive, and it is our role to create such an environment. Here are some ways whereby we can achieve this:

- Consistency in our coaching approach. This means we need to coach all students with the same diligence and enthusiasm. If we are in a group class environment, we cannot reserve our best coaching efforts for the students we more easily relate too.

- Always being respectful with our students. Being a trainer or coach does not give us the freedom to directly or indirectly insult, make fun of, or berate our students.

- Caring about our students. Watching for signs of frustration or lack of motivation. Always providing an empathetic approach and helping guide them to any additional resources they may need.

- Remaining flexible and finding creative and fun ways to encourage, motivate and reward effort and results.

- Being a cheerleader for our students and celebrating their successes, even the small ones.

Create a Trusting Environment

Whether in training sessions or elsewhere clients will sometimes initiate discussions on sensitive topics, which is normal in a coach-trainee relationship. If clients open up to us, it demonstrates that they trust us. As their coach, establishing and maintaining trust is the most essential ingredient to the entire process. If trust is not present in the relationship, our advice or guidance may be viewed with skepticism. However, building trust with clients requires us to invest time and effort in the relationship, given that they will usually not trust us from the outset.

Training and coaching sessions should never be used to deliver bad news, negative feedback, complaints or criticism about the training program, client or the process. Discussions that are unlikely to be viewed positively by the client, or do not actually involve hands-on learning, should be scheduled separately. It should go without saying that professional trainers should never degrade students or use negative words to describe them, such as "lazy" or "uncommitted." In group class environments, we must never shun difficult clients or treat them differently. Punishment does not belong in coaching or training sessions, and nor do evaluations where the performance of differing family members are discussed or debated. Sessions should be a safe haven and provide an encouraging, fun environment. To accelerate the development of trust with clients, here are a few tips:

- Maintain and take advantage of positive body language.
- Listen to students and really understand what they are saying.
- Always respect students.
- Keep all information confidential.
- Make and keep promises.
- Always be honest and transparent.
- Be confident about who you are and what you have to offer.
- Instill belief in the client's abilities to work through the

program by demonstrating that you believe in them.

- Recognize obstacles when they appear and help clients overcome them, whether they are physical or social, or relating to safety or self- esteem.

The System - On Task Skill Coaching

Why does on task skill coaching work so well? Simply stated, the learning cycle involves moving from experience, to reflecting, to conceptualizing and, finally, to integrating the actual skills. On Task Skill Coaching has been developed around this theory and is a practical application of Experiential Learning:

1. As we are learning, we first **experience** something new and immerse ourselves in it. We bring our own biases to the experience so we are caught up in our own individual meanings.

2. Next, we **reflect** on the experience. We begin to filter it through our own eyes based on our past experiences. As we move through this reflection we are able to dismiss our biases and rigidity to see and feel more objectively what we have just experienced.

3. Then we **conceptualize**, at which point we narrow our focus from individual reflections and move from

perception to concept. We seek to understand what we have experienced so we can label it or classify it in a way that makes sense to us based on our previous experiences.

4. Finally, we take **action** once we understand the concept. For most of us though, action is not enough. We need to play around with the experience, tweak it and make it work for us. At this stage we have become part of the manipulation process. In other words, we can manipulate our actions based on our experiences, reflections and conceptualizations.

These four components, experience, reflection, conceptualization and action, are the four cornerstones of professor of organizational behavior and educational theorist David A. Kolb's Experiential Learning Cycle.

Figure 4-1: Kolb's Experiential Learning Cycle

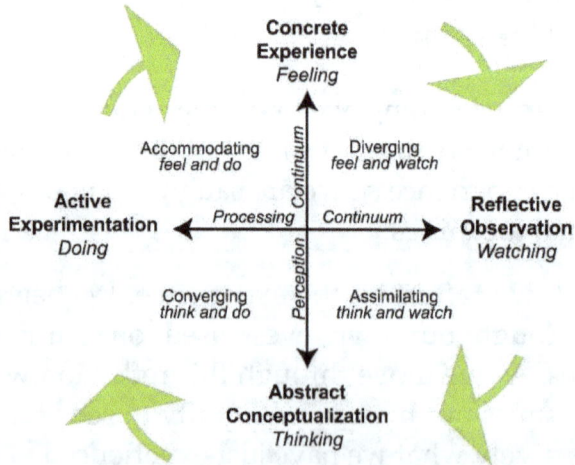

The System – On Task Skill Coaching

Consider the learning cycle as made up of quadrants (*see Figure 4-1*). In the first quadrant, the individual is limited by the boundaries of their experience and the resulting reflection. McCarthy (2006, p. 23) presents that we are answering the question "why?" in this quadrant. At this stage, students are discovering personal meaning and making connections based on their own experiences.

In the second quadrant, students are moving from experience to conceptualization through reflection. In other words, they are experiencing the "what." This involves classifying, comparing, patterning and organizing all the information.

In the third quadrant, students are restricted by the boundaries of abstract conceptualization and active experimentation. They are experiencing the "how." They are beginning to move from knowledge to practical implementation, and are practicing and testing accuracy. At this stage, students are working towards mastery through doing, questioning and comparing results.

In the fourth quadrant, students are at last bound by active experimentation and concrete experience. They are able to refine what they have learned and integrate it into their daily lives. This quadrant represents the "if." Students will be able to establish for themselves how they can use their new skills in unique and varied ways, and will be celebrating their new-found competencies and improved performance. This is exactly where, as trainers, we would like our students to be.

Ultimately, when the On Task Skill Coaching method is executed correctly, it will help students navigate their way around the learning cycle so they learn more effectively from their experiences with us, as trainers, and are better able to transfer everything they have learned to their respective real-life scenarios.

Our goal as professional trainers is to impart as much knowledge to our students as we can, supported by new and effective training skills, so we are no longer useful or necessary. If we are to do this, then we must be effective at teaching them to train their pets to a high level of competency.

If we study the graphic in Figure 4-1, we can see, during each step, which part of the learning cycle the student is passing through and how it is impacting their experience. Learning is a continuous process.

Beard and Wilson (2013) maintain that "we do not learn from experience, we learn from reflecting on experience," and, during training sessions, it is important to facilitate this reflection with our students. According to Kolb's Experiential Learning Cycle (2015), new knowledge is attained through a combination of perceiving and processing. Here are the four complete states in the cycle:

1. *Concrete Experience* - this experience can be planned or accidental. (Perceiving Line).

2. *Reflective Observation* - thinking about the experience and its significance to individual students. (Processing Line).

3. *Abstract Conceptualization* (*i.e. Theorizing*) - generalizing from experience to similar situations. (Perceiving Line).

4. *Active Experimentation* - testing ideas generated from the experience in new situations. The cycle then starts again. (Processing Line).

As we teach our students, we must recognize they will go through a process whereby they must decide, consciously or not, whether they want to learn by doing or by watching. Simultaneously, they must consider whether to think or feel. Kolb (2015) calls this "dialectically related modes" of "grasping experience" (doing or watching) and "transforming experience" (feeling or thinking). The process of On Task Skill Coaching ensures students go through all the necessary stages to learn effectively, so they are able to use the skills and knowledge acquired.

In summary, students' immediate experiences in the learning environment form the basis for their individual observations and reflections. These are refined into abstract concepts, with students taking on new information under advisement. This is then actively tested and used to form guidelines for future experiences.

The On Task Skill Coaching Method

We are now ready to examine what we might call our training recipe. This is the formula we use to facilitate clients or students moving accurately and effectively through the learning cycle.

By this stage, we should already have completed our functional assessment and have all the requisite information to develop the training plan, as well as an outline of the road map, i.e. the training program journey, we will be traveling with the client to solve the behavior problem(s) and reach the agreed goal(s).

Key Deliverables from the Functional Assessment:

1. A description of the behavior problem using applied

behavior analysis terminology, and a contingency statement showing the three- or two- term contingency.

2. A hypothesis of what is going on with a high rate of confidence.

3. A goal statement or statements agreed on by all parties.

4. A program outline including:

   a. Management tools and activities – this includes a plan for implementing management tools to prevent exposure to the problematic conditioned stimulus and to address any other safety concerns (if applicable).

   b. Training Skills - we should know what we need to teach in terms of individual skills and any equipment needed to facilitate this.

   c. Relationship Exercises - there should be a plan to address relationship-building activities if there is a deficit of trust from previous training and care practices.

   d. Behavior Change Protocols – if we are embarking on a full-blown behavior change program, we must make sure our contingency statement identifies the problematic antecedent so we can begin the counterconditioning program.

The goal of the On Task Skill Coaching system is to help pet professionals determine exactly what knowledge needs to be transferred to clients to support the hands-on training sessions. The various moving parts of the training program should have been taken care of during the approach and planning steps discussed in section one, *The Approach*.

We are now going to cover:

1. The Training Road Map – the high-level plan of the program, lessons and sessions.

2. The Training Lesson Plans - how many lessons do we think we need to plan for, and what will we cover in each lesson? How will we progressively teach the various skills so they make the most sense in terms of meeting the client's needs?

3. The Lesson Session Plans – in each lesson we may have between three to five individual training sessions. What will these look like and how will we execute them?

The Road Map

The road map should contain all the necessary elements required to build a training plan. These will be broken down into a lesson plan and then individual session plans, i.e. micro training sessions within each lesson. They do not necessarily have to be in order of priority or have a structure, but they are the components we have determined as essential for the training program to be successful.

These components include:

- *Specific training skills.*
- *Management tools and activities.*
- *Relationship building exercises.*
- *Counterconditioning elements.*

Key Training Plan Objectives for the Road Map

Sample Behavior Problem: Leash Reactivity

Objective One – Prepare the dog and owner with the skills and equipment they need to safely go on walks while avoiding, whenever possible, the problematic conditioned stimulus. This way physical exercise and mental enrichment will not be compromised.

Objective Two – Reframe the canine-human bond by developing a more collegial relationship. Introduce some fun and easy activities that can take place between the dog and owner, such as play and games that will develop a strong reinforcement history. Those who play together, stay together. These types of activities will also be very useful during any counterconditioning program to help maintain a relaxed and fun environment and approach.

Objective Three – Commence with a counterconditioning program the owner can competently work with in the absence of the trainer.

Objective Four – Develop the necessary training ability and knowledge to mastery level so the owner has the skills for life, and learning is fun for all concerned.

The top priority in this particular training plan is to develop the skills and tools needed to help the owner be able to take the dog for walks around the neighborhood. Leash walking skills are addressed first, and supported by fun games and relationship-building activities.

These are the key objectives for the plan, and although it may run for 10 weeks or more, there are no guarantees. We can certainly talk to our clients about our road map and all the deliverables we need for success but we cannot guarantee results. How quickly the training progresses will be based on the allocation and completion of homework, which is contingent on the client's commitment and compliance with the program.

The Training Lesson Plan

The training plan is developed from the training road map and will highlight the order of priority in terms of what to address and when.

I have detailed a sample training plan in Figure 4-2 on pages 75 and 76. In it, I have provided an outline of priorities over a six-week period for instructional purposes. Note that there is a reason why the activities on the plan have been placed in a certain order for this specific case:

   a. The dog has leash reactivity problems with large men at a distance of 20 feet, moving or stationary, so the plan will incorporate systematic desensitization and counterconditioning.

   b. The dog has no current obedience behaviors that are under stimulus control (i.e. no sit, wait, down, walk nicely, etc.).

   c. The dog's problematic behavior has been maintained through negative reinforcement. The dog's operant behaviors of barking and lunging are elicited through fear, a conditioned emotional response. This behavior has worked for the dog, either because the stimulus perceived to be a threat has always removed itself from view, or the dog's owner has removed the dog from the situation. Both consequences have resulted in removal of the aversive stimulus.

d. The dog is only 9 months old and has no bite or fight history with other dogs. Indeed, no problems at all have been noted with other dogs.

e. The dog has no bite history with people. A muzzle was introduced to the plan to provide mental and visual comfort for an overly anxious owner who currently has no leash handling skills.

f. The owner stipulated emphatically in the goal statement that they not only wanted a dog that no longer reacted to strange men but also demonstrated a high degree of obedience around the home and on walks.

Figure 4-2: The Six-Week Training Plan Detailing Skills and Theory

Session #	Location	Knowledge (Teaching Theory)	Skills (Training Mechanics)

1	Client home (2-hour session)	• Review current cues and skill levels
		• Overview of training philosophy
		  • Management - purpose
		  • Training - how
		  • Relationship - why
		• Review equipment use
		• Theory of name game, hand feeding and mental stimulation exercises
		• Theory for including play
		• Theory for using harness
		• Practical application of new skills
		• Kongs and toys – purpose and use
			• Clicker mechanics, timing and purpose
			• Hand feeding exercise
			• Name game process
			• Play activities
			• Fitting and desensitizing a harness
			• Practical application and context of new skills
			• Practical application of Kongs and toys

2	Client home (2-hour session)	• Theory of muzzle training • Theory of crate training • Theory of "let's go" • Theory of leash walking	• Recap of homework • Muzzle training • Crate training • Let's go • Walk nicely
3	Client home (1-hour session)	• Theory of sit and down acquisition • Theory of maintain	• Recap of homework • Sit/down • Maintain

4	Client home and quiet area outdoors (1-hour session)	• Theory of counterconditioning and desensitization • Recap on leash walking – Oops, what do I do now	• Practice trials • Practice trials

5	Client home and quiet area outdoors (1-hour session)	• Theory of relax
		• Recap of counterconditioning and desensitization Recap of sit/down/maintain
			• Relax game practice (end of session)
			• Review of crate training
			• On the road
			  • Let's go
			  • Play with tug toys
			  • Leash walking
			  • Sit/down/maintain
			  • Counterconditioning exercises

6	Outdoor area with light traffic and exposure to the problematic conditioned stimulus (1-hour session)	• Recap theory of counterconditioning • Recap theory or conditioned relax	On the road • Counterconditioning exercises • Practical application of let's go, • sit/down maintain

Teaching versus Training

You may be wondering why I have divided the tasks in Figure 4-2 between teaching and training. Upon examination of the literature discussing the topic of teaching versus training, it becomes apparent that teaching is theoretically oriented, whereas training has more of a practical application. Teaching facilitates new knowledge. Training, on the other hand, helps those who already have the knowledge to learn the tools and techniques required to apply that knowledge. Teaching penetrates minds while training shapes habits and skills. Teachers provide information and knowledge while trainers facilitate learning. Or, as Clay H. Trumbull (1890) states: "It has been said that the essence of teaching is causing another to know." It may similarly be said that "the essence of training is causing another to do." (Rao, 2008).

Training is an interactive activity that helps us to perform skills. It requires learning by doing and experiencing practical activities (Pollice, 2003). In my opinion, and stated across the relevant literature, training focuses on skills and narrows the focus, possibly over a shorter period of time. Typically, we also associate training with repetitive learning until we achieve skill competency and the skill becomes second nature. A select review of the literature discussing teaching suggests that, in contrast to training, the search of, or transfer of knowledge is deeper and broader, and takes place over a longer period of time. We often say learning is a lifelong occupation.

Essentially, the goals associated with teaching and training are different. I am not suggesting these roles are mutually exclusive and it is important we balance our roles between teaching and transferring knowledge, and training and getting the job done. We must help and support our clients so they can help and support and facilitate their pets' learning.

I conclude here that training is a subset of teaching. Figure 4-3 highlights some of the topics that we, within our scope as trainers and behavior consultants, touch on when teaching our clients. In the figure, I have differentiated between topics that require skill training, or hands-on competency, and those that require teaching, or the transfer of knowledge. I think it is fair to say that the majority of these activities would be best taught alongside the skill training exercises.

Figure 4-3: Skill Training vs. Knowledge Teaching

Examples of Skill Training
To train = to form by instruction, to make prepared for a kill.
○ Obedience skills – sit, down, walk nicely etc. ○ Luring skills – mechanics, timing. ○ Shaping skills – mechanics, timing. ○ Key management skills – crate training etc. ○ Husbandry skills – grooming, ear cleaning. ○ Relationship-building skills – hand feeding.

The System - On Task Skill Coaching

Examples of Knowledge Teaching
To teach = to cause to know something, to guide the studies, impart the knowledge, to instruct.

- Elements of safety, position, product
- knowledge, tools and equipment.
- Overview of canine enrichment, needs,
- exercise requirements, nurturing.
- Canine communication.
- The theory of skill acquisition, proofing, and
- generalization.
- Theory of luring, fading of lure, transferal of
- cue, reinforcement theory.
- Crate training criteria.

The Individual Sessions

This area focuses on the individual sessions within a training lesson, which is the period of time we are contracted to provide training services to our clients. A lesson may contain several short training sessions on separate and/or interrelated topics. We need to make sure we run these sessions as effectively as possible.

Most of our lessons are service products that we sell. They are generally one hour long, or sold in increments of one hour. We may even package them so clients can buy them in groups, in which case they are usually prepaid and qualify for a small prepay discount, either for group training or individual sessions.

We will now look at a typical lesson plan taken from our Six-Week Training Plan (*detailed in Figure 4-2*).

Before we arrive at the client's home we need to have any important documents ready and make sure we have all the relevant training equipment. Preparation is essential. It is very unprofessional to arrive at a training appointment and then realize we have forgotten the muzzle or handout we need to conduct the lesson effectively. However, if it does happen, we have one of two choices: a) omit that skill session from the lesson, or b) train the skill without all the necessary tools. Neither of these options is conducive to getting outstanding training results. I firmly believe that, if training is to be professional and effective, it needs to be done correctly, and that means having all the necessary tools and documents on hand and prepared.

During our preparation we need to try to picture the actual training lesson and the planned sessions. What are the individual training tasks we will focus on? What will we say, and how will we explain the "how," "what" and "why" of our training plan? How will we demonstrate the actual skill? What questions do we anticipate the client will ask and how will we answer them? How will we handle any problems that may arise?

Finally, we must be sure we completely understand our material so we can competently demonstrate everything we expect the client to learn. We cannot just wing it when teaching a paying client. This would be highly irresponsible and very unprofessional.

The System - On Task Skill Coaching

Quick Preparation Checklist

1. Do we have your training road map?
2. Do we have our training plan?
3. Have we prepared our individual lesson plan?
4. How many skills session do we plan to execute in the lesson?
5. Do we have our skill sessions planned? This means:

    a. Do we know what we will teach first and to what criteria?

    b. Have we developed our how, what and why?

    c. Do we have the necessary handouts to support knowledge transfer in conjunction with the skill training we have planned?

    d. Do we have all the correct equipment on hand?

    e. Are we dressed appropriately, i.e. do we look professional?

The individual lesson plan document in Figure 4-4 highlights an example of an individual lesson from the six-week training plan. The lesson is then dissected into two components:

1. What knowledge will we be transferring to the client?
2. What skills will we need to teach the client so they can train their dog competently?

In addition, we must identify what supporting documents are required for the knowledge transfer and what equipment is needed for the skill training. When training the skills what criteria do we hope to achieve? When we have multiple clients it is important to record this information so we know, when we arrive for a lesson, where we left off, where the client stands, and where this lesson plans to take us.

Before we begin any individual training sessions within a lesson, we should be very clear about what exactly we will be training and to what criteria. Using a lesson plan like the one detailed in Figure 4-4 helps us to be sure we have all the necessary support and homework documentation.

Note that in the lesson plan there is a column for goal criteria. This will ensure we know the exact criteria each skill will be trained to in any individual lesson.

The System – On Task Skill Coaching

Figure 4-4: Individual Lesson Plan Highlighting the Supporting Documentation Needed and Goal Criteria for the Skills Being Covered

Knowledge (Teaching Theory)	Supporting Documents	Four Skill Sessions	Goal Criteria

• Overview of training philosophy
• Review equipment use
• Theory of name game, hand feeding and mental stimulation exercises
• Theory for including play
• Theory for using harness
• Practical application of new skills
• Kongs and toys – purpose and use
	• Handouts on training versus management versus relationships
	• Handouts on each of the following skills:
	  • play
	  • harnesses vs. collars
	  • Kong filler recipes
		1. Using a clicker, mechanics, timing and purpose
		2. Relationship Exercises
		  • Hand feeding exercise
		  • Name game process
		  • Play activities
		3. Fitting and desensitizing a harness
		4. Filling a Kong toy
			• Charging the clicker, timing, position and treat delivery
			• Hand feeding for seven days while playing the name game and making positive eye contact
			• Identifying two play activities for inside the house and two for the yard
			• Dressing and undressing the dog with a harness while eliciting a conditioned emotional response
			• Three Kongs prepped for use

As discussed previously, we may have three to five individual skill training sessions within one lesson, and we need to prepare for each one of them. As can be seen in Figure 4-4, there are multiple sessions in each single lesson.

Each lesson should be conducted in the same way. This entails working to the same method every time to ensure we guide students through the Experiential Learning Cycle. There is a formula for this and I will now present an overview of the various steps involved, as well as what should be covered in each lesson.

The On Task Skill Coaching System has eight steps (*see Figure 4-5*). The separate components of the individual session are as follows:

- Open the session.
- Show the finished skill.
- One-way demonstration.
- Two-way demonstration.
- Trainee performs the task.
- Supervised student practice.
- Wrap up session.
- Assign homework.

Figure 4.5: The On Task Skill Coaching Process

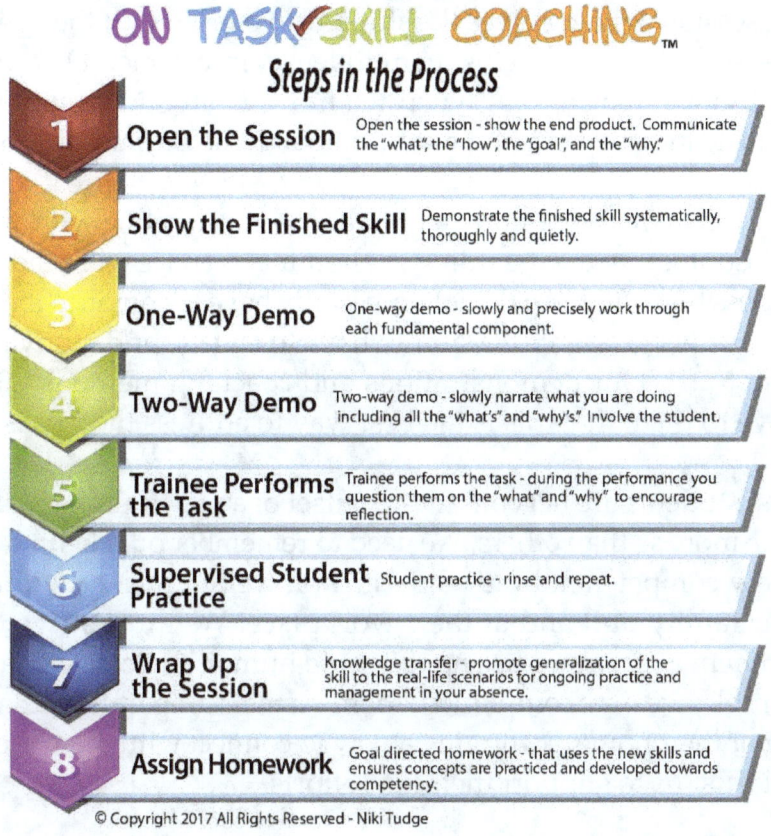

Figure 4.6 on pages 88-90 details a sample session planning worksheet to explain the On Task Skill Coaching Process and the individual components.

We will now examine each section of On Skill Task Coaching and its role in the overall method.

Step 1: Open the Session

The session opening gives the student an overview of the overall session plan and helps them to feel comfortable. It should be obvious to a student when we move from one session to another, and not just a blur of multiple activities within a lesson.

If we have a nervous student or one who is struggling with any philosophical issues regarding the training, then we will need to address these first. We do not necessarily have to convince them that our way is right. We simply have to engage and motivate them to try. Our demonstrations and coaching methods will prove to them that this is the best way to address the issues.

Most students are nervous at the outset of a new training plan, some more so than others. We need to remember our clients are highly competent adults who function well in society, within their family unit and at their workplace. We must strive to put them at ease and use appropriate humor if necessary. For example, we may compliment them on their preparation, their dog or their home. By finding a way to connect with them they will trust us to support their first efforts.

At the beginning of each new session we introduce the skill we will be covering. It is important to be very specific. If we have formal goals for a particular session, this is when we will review them.

Keep this opening as short as possible. It may be as simple as saying: "For our first training session within the lesson, we are going to teach [resident dog] Jack how to sit." In fact, we are

The System – On Task Skill Coaching

not going to teach him how to sit at all as he knows how to do that already. Rather, we are going to teach him to sit when we politely request him to do so. By the end of this first session, our goal is for Jack to sit on request to a verbal cue and/or a hand signal for up to five seconds. If we think back to when we discussed impulse control around doors and guests, this will really help with any issue like that. How wonderful would it be if the client can ask Jack to sit while they are carrying the baby and trying to open the door? In our session we will teach Jack using the capturing method and reinforcing all the right behaviors. This makes it fun for him and fun for us too. We are going to make training a game for him so he wants to learn and at the same time we all get to feel good about each other.

During the opening segment of each session we will discuss:

— What we are going to be training. We need to create an expectation, paint the picture, explain the vision and generate interest and excitement.

— The goal criteria we plan to reach. This involves identifying to the client where the milestone will be for this particular session versus the complete skill. Our goal is tangible and clear, in this case a duration of up to five seconds via a hand signal or verbal cue.

— Why we are training this particular skill in this particular way. Adults in particular need to understand the relevance of what and why we are training what we are training. We have shown them that using the capturing method is fun for Jack and fun for us. We can make it a game for everyone.

Figure 4.6: The Session Planning Worksheet

Step 1 Open the session	Open the session. Introduce your session title. Keep it short and salient - just a quick introduction on the what, the goal, the how and the why.
Session name (i.e. what are you teaching?)	What is your session name and what is the student going to learn? *Example: We will be teaching a sit behavior with a short duration dimension.*
Goal (SMART)	Specific, Measurable, Attainable, Result Driven and Timeline agreed. *Example: The dog will "sit," i.e. place his rump on the ground when we use the cue "sit" or the hand signal for "sit." The dog will remain in that "sit" position for up to five seconds with the client standing in front of the dog.*
How? (key method, philosophy)	Explain how you will achieve the behavior via your method of choice. *Example: We will be capturing the behavior and rewarding each "sit" the dog offers. When the dog's rump hits the ground, we will say "yes" and give him a treat.*
Why? (relevance must be identified)	Why does your student need to learn this and why learn it in this specific manner? Make it relevant to them. *Example: We are going to capture behaviors so we do not need to use food in our hands to lure the behavior as Jack is a little grabby around food. Teaching Jack to "sit" on cue when we request it will help us move on to impulse control exercises next. This will help you manage Jack around doors and food, the reason you embarked on the training lessons.*
Notes for the session (your thoughts and observations)	

The System – On Task Skill Coaching

Step 2 - 8	Items to prepare and have on hand	Sequence of events – key points to keep you on track	
Step 2 Demonstrate the finished skill systematically, thoroughly and quietly.	• Treat bag. • Small moist treats. • A harness and leash. • A squeaky toy.	• Use the squeaky toy to attract Jack. • Use the toy movement to lure Jack into a "sit." • Mark when the rump is in position by saying "yes." • Deliver reinforcement. • Use the reinforcement to reset Jack so another trial can be captured.	
Step 3 One-Way Demo - slowly and precisely work through each fundamental component.		*Key mechanics, timing and equipment to focus on.* • This time you will do everything in slow motion so the trainee can see every one of your mechanics and mark points. • Emphasize lure motion, marker, and reinforcement delivery.	
Step 4 Two-Way Demo – slowly narrate what you are doing, including all the what's and why's. Involve the student.		*What's and why's identified with each point.*	
		What's	Why's
		Explain role of the toy to lure.	Why use a toy.
		Explain marker position.	Why mark now.
		Explain reinforcement delivery.	Why deliver treat in that location.

Step 5 Trainee performs the task – during the performance you question them on the what and the why to encourage reflection.		*What questions will you ask the student during the performance?*
		Why do you deliver the food in this way? How do we define a sit?
Step 6 Student practice. Rinse and repeat. Coach. Rinse and repeat. Coach.		*Identify potential coaching points and how to address them.*
		When you are watching your student, analyze what meets the training criteria and what needs improvement for both the pet and the human student.
		Improve and work on one point at a time. Do a few trials of getting the marker correct, then maybe work on the reinforcement delivery if both of those aspects need attention.
Step 7 Wrap up the session - knowledge transfer		*How will you generalize and transfer knowledge on this skill?*
		Talk to your student about how they can generalize the behavior in different areas. How can they use this new behavior and integrate it into everyday situations?
Step 8 Homework assignment	What handouts do you need with you?	*What homework will be assigned (both principles and practice)?*
		What will you assign as homework? Make sure all assigned homework has been coached so you know the student can complete it competently.

Step 2: Show the Finished Skill

During this phase, we will fully demonstrate the skill up to the criteria determined by our goal. The goal is to demonstrate the finished product to the student so they get an opportunity

The System - On Task Skill Coaching

to observe and conceptualize what they are about to learn. If this will take more than a couple of minutes, we are planning too much for this micro session. We should not have students sitting or standing watching us for too long as they may become bored and lose focus and motivation.

Another goal during this phase is to show the student exactly how the skill should be completed. If we cannot complete the entire session in 10 minutes, then we probably need to break it down into smaller components and plan more sessions. For example, I would not schedule teaching a student the sit behavior with both a distance and duration dimension in a single session. This would be too much for one session and would confuse the student. Remember, we can have multiple sessions in one lesson. I am not suggesting we could not cover this in one lesson; I am suggesting it would be best trained in different or concurrent sessions.

While we are demonstrating a new skill we need to be careful not to confuse the student by altering how we train it. This means demonstrating one method fully. For example, if we are capturing sits and marking them with a clicker and then jump to luring, we will confuse the student. We need to choose our method and stick to it until the student has accomplished that skill in that session. The exception to this would be if we have a dog that is not offering the target behavior for reinforcement. In this situation we would need to move to a different method and offer a more guided approach to learning. If, however, we are well-prepared and have had some interaction with the dog prior to our first lesson, we should be able to predict and work around these types of problems.

When taking students through the demonstration, we must bear in mind we are not a mirror. It may be easier in some cases for them to watch from behind or to the side.

By showing the client the end result we will motivate them to try out the skill for themselves. They will see how the behavior will be in the future and this can very quickly reframe the relationship they have with their dog.

Step 3: The One-Way Demo

Next we will demonstrate the skill very slowly without editorializing each component. We need to let the student watch carefully, and follow these guidelines:

- Check we have everything we need on hand, including:
    - The dog wearing the correct equipment.
    - Our clicker or marker.
    - Our choice of reinforcement.
- Position ourselves and the dog so the student can fully see what we are doing.
- Work slowly and methodically.
- If the student needs to observe from a different angle, repeat from a different orientation.
- Complete the full skill as per the goal.

Step 4: The Two-Way Demo

Effective trainers demonstrate twice minimum. Demonstrating helps cement the training in the working memory and facilitates the learning cycle. In the two-way demo we are involving our student. They are thinking and looking at what we are doing.

The System - On Task Skill Coaching

They should be engaged by the session.

At the beginning of the session we will do a quick recap of what we are training in the session and why we are training it. Then, for each step of the actual mechanical hands-on process, we need to focus on the "how" (*see Figure 4-7*).

When we present the various training tools to the student, it helps to have a spare set so we are not passing equipment back and forth (e.g. clickers, training pouches, treats.) If necessary, we will allow the student to make a closer inspection or try them out.

- For example:
    - The clicker - allow the student to touch, feel and hear the clicker. (The clicker should already be a conditioned reinforcer, which would have been a separate session).
    - The dog - give an overview of the dog's starting position and any equipment he is wearing.
    - The type of reinforcement, size, consistency, position of pouch, and quantity to be delivered for each correct response, as well as reinforcement delivery position.

We will now demonstrate the exact same skill again, only this time we will slowly explain what we are doing, step by step. It is important to engage the student during the demonstration and, if relevant, ask them questions about what we are doing. We need to stress key points, such as commitment points, marker points and reinforcement delivery.

Caution: Avoid information overload. Training students is not about showing them how much we know; rather it is about showing them enough to enable them to master the task. It is essential not overwhelm them with information, handouts and industry nomenclature.

The "How" Explained

During the second demonstration, we will get to the "how." We will explain everything as we are doing it and why we are doing it this way, paying attention to the following:

- The position of any lures, if we are providing guided learning (why).
- The location of our body and hands, the clicker, and the reinforcement (why).
- The mechanics of the dog's body as he moves into the skill position (why).
- The point of commitment (why).
- The point of marking (why).
- The delivery of the reinforcement (why).

For someone who has not previously been involved in training a dog, some of these things may seem a little strange. It is not obvious to a student why we do – or do not – do certain things. For this reason, we need to point them out as we go along so students gain a high degree of understanding of the skill and the method of training, as well as why it is trained in this particular way.

If we do this effectively then, even in our absence, our students will be able to choose to train correctly and to the model we have provided. Students can thus perform their practice sessions correctly, which sets up both them and their dogs for success.

Figure 4-7: Examples of What, How and Why in Training the Sit Behavior

What	How	Why
Timing of the clicker.	Click when the dog's rump hits the ground.	The click is a promise to pay. It tells the dog precisely what he is getting paid for. If we click too early then we are reinforcing whatever behavior the dog is engaging in at that moment. What is reinforced will be repeated.
Lure mechanics.	Position the lure on a magical piece of string just in front of the dog's nose.	The correct position of the lure will determine the effectiveness of the luring. It should be positioned so we can encourage the dog's movement in whatever direction we are looking for. Take care not to move it too slowly – which may create a mouthing problem – or too quickly, whereby the dog loses interest.
Position of reinforcement.	Reinforce the dog by delivering the treat while the dog is in position.	Reward the dog in position as this will strengthen the behavior and the effectiveness of the reinforcing experience.

Step 5: Trainee Performs the Task

It is now time to have the trainee perform the task and

practice what we have demonstrated. First, we take them through a review of what has happened so they can begin to evaluate the task after engaging in the process with us. We need to:

- Ask the student to describe the process they have watched in as much detail as they can remember.
- Ask specific questions about the process that we feel are particularly salient. Some examples are:
  - At what point did I click?
  - Where was the dog positioned when I delivered the treat?
  - How long after the dog's butt hit the floor did I click?
  - Was I restraining the dog?
  - Did the dog look happy?

This will probably be the most difficult time for us as trainers. The student is going to begin practicing the new skill. We must try not to be anxious if they get it wrong or make a mistake. This is about the experience, and they need to experience the event to learn. Mistakes can help with reflection and conceptualizing what they are actually doing if the learning environment is safe. If they veer off course, we are going to be very tempted to jump in. We cannot. It can unnerve students and make them feel inadequate. We will only step in if we absolutely MUST, because what they are doing is having unpleasant and unintended consequences for them or the dog.

We must remember that we will have to communicate the

The System - On Task Skill Coaching

"why" to many of these "how's." When students ask why we are doing it this way, we do not want to appear stumped if we have not thought about it or if we just do not know. Preparation is mission critical.

If at all possible we must let the student finish the task first but we must always be prepared for questions. As soon as the student finishes we need to:

- Acknowledge they have completed the task.

- Describe to them in a very constructive manner what was done well and what we think could be improved upon.

- Ask them how they felt about what they were doing and what they achieved.

- Ask them what they feel they can improve on.

- Ask them about their overall experience.

- Recap areas needing adjustment. If there are more than one, then choose the most important one to focus on in the next trial.

  - *We cannot expect to be able to tell students their clicker timing was off, their body position was wrong and their reinforcement delivery was slow, and expect them to get all three things right in the next trial. First, it will just not happen and, second, our feedback will feel unsupportive and may also be demotivating. We must coach and adjust one step at a time.*

- Rinse and repeat until the skill is solid and the student can perform it seamlessly.

- At this juncture, we may choose to add another dimension

to the behavior, such as duration, distance or distractions. By doing it this way, students are only required to learn one new criteria, i.e. when to click and treat, as an incremental learning step.

Step 6: Supervised Practice

We will continue supporting the student's practice until we are satisfied they can do it correctly and comfortably. During this time we will be engaged in the process of observing, encouraging and coaching our students, and helping them make tweaks and changes to their technique so they can master the task. We may also need to supplement their theoretical knowledge so they can better conceptualize what they are learning.

Coaching is only helpful if it provides students with exactly what they need to know in a courteous and upbeat manner. To accelerate the learning of difficult components, we can have students practice problem areas in individual sessions. Their practice needs to be both goal oriented and sufficiently challenging. Practicing is not just about time on the task but about the quality of the practice. Trainers need to supervise practice until the student understands all the moving parts. Incorrect practice will impede skill building, which is why it is so important we observe them doing the skill correctly before we consider assigning any homework.

Step 7: Wrap Up the Session

The practice sessions are more useful if we wrap them up appropriately. This means talking to the client about how these new skills can and should be used in everyday real settings. This facilitates knowledge transfer. Knowledge transfer

The System – On Task Skill Coaching

comprises the application of skills and knowledge from the training environment to real life scenarios. To effect transfer, students need to understand the mechanics. This transfer is most easily completed if the learning context is similar to the real-life context, for example training pet dogs in their home environment or setting up group classes to resemble real-life situations.

When wrapping up each session we can ask additional questions to help students further evaluate and review what they have learned. Here is a list of potential questions from the review session, which typically lasts around 10 minutes:

- In terms of building a duration behavior where do you think you should go now? What duration criteria can you click for?

- How can you practice this behavior without having to set up specific practice sessions?

- During the dog's everyday life, when can you ask for a sit and what secondary reinforcers can you deliver for a prompt behavior?

Step 8: Assign Homework

Homework can now be assigned from this individual session or based on the lesson framework. We need to decide which is best based on the client, how much we have covered, and what is important. I only set homework based on skills I have coached students through and have seen them practice correctly. That way we both know that, when I leave their home or we end the session, they have the full competency to practice the skill correctly. For example, for a sit behavior I would need to be sure that they know:

— The correct luring mechanics.

— The correct clicker timing.

— The reinforcement delivery position and reinforcement schedule.

— How to build on the criteria. This means that if we had achieved a three-second sit, I need to know by way of demonstration that my student knows how to build on this to achieve a 20-second sit.

I also need to be sure they can practice this every day within the scope of the dog's normal management and care. It is best if practice is goal directed and has targeted feedback. This way it promotes the best learning gains and we can collectively achieve our training goals for the pet, the owner and the professional.

Implementation

Figure 4-8 demonstrates how On Task Skill Coaching meets the Experiential Learning Cycle. By implementing this simple and effective system you can become a highly effective trainer of people. You will be overjoyed by the results you see, results that will positively impact the lives of pet dogs and their owners daily. From your informant interview process and the way you functionally analyze behavior to your lesson and session planning, you will find engaged and motivated students who effectively capture and retain your teachings.

Figure 4-8: How On Task Skill Coaching Meets the Learning Cycle

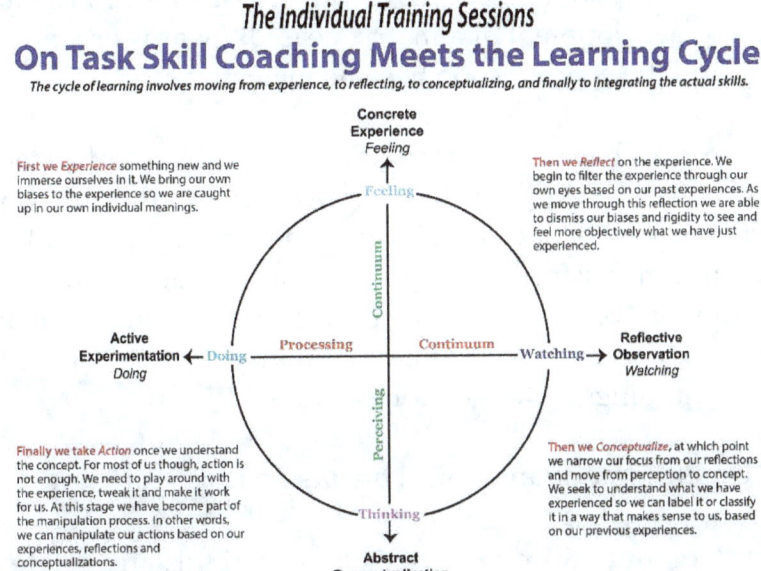

Before you move on from this book, take a moment to make a few notes on the key things you have learned that you feel will be beneficial to implement in your business. Next, prioritize the tasks, schedule them in your calendar and begin to work on them. Don't let work or being busy stop you from making fundamental changes to your existing processes if you determine there is a need for improvement.

In a 1954 speech to the Second Assembly of the World Council of Churches, President Dwight Eisenhower, who was quoting Dr. J. Roscoe Miller, president of Northwestern University in Chicago, Illinois, said: "I have two kinds of problems: the urgent and the important. The urgent are not important, and the important are never urgent."

In his book, *The Seven Habits of Highly Effective People*, Steven Covey (1994) popularized this so-called Eisenhower Principle with the development of a matrix geared towards organizing tasks, and the concept soon became mainstream.

Many people have a tendency to work on whatever has most recently landed on their desk, answer emails, or focus on a specific task someone is pressuring them to complete. I hear so often from business consulting students that they have no time to work on their goals or projects because they are just so busy. They are so busy working on urgent matters that the important things never get done.

The Urgent/Important Matrix breaks up tasks as follows:

- **Urgent and Important:** Activities in this area relate to dealing with critical issues as they arise and meeting significant commitments. *Perform these duties now.*

- **Important but Not Urgent:** These success-oriented tasks are critical to achieving goals. *Plan to do these tasks next.*

- **Urgent but Not Important**: These impositions do not move you forward toward your own goals. Manage them by delaying them, cutting them short and rejecting requests from other people. *Postpone these.*

- **Not Urgent and Not Important:** These trivial interruptions are just a distraction. *Avoid these distractions altogether.*

The System - On Task Skill Coaching

> *Important versus Urgent*
>
> **Important:** These are activities that lead you to achieving your goals and have the greatest impact on your life.
>
> **Urgent:** These activities demand immediate attention but will not contribute to long-term goals or activities. They are often a burden placed on you by others.

Projects can often be so overwhelming it is difficult to get them started. Or, because they are so overwhelming, and if we do not have a time management system, we work on them from start to finish so the reminder of our business life falls into disarray. Think about teaching new behaviors to students and dogs. We always say break things down into several steps. Do not expect to achieve everything at once. If we take a similar approach, we can work progressively on our large projects and goals.

First of all, divide your new project into manageable chunks. Then you can block off time in your calendar to work on it. Once the time is allocated make sure you stick to it. For example, when I decided to write this book the first thing I did was develop my outline. Then I scheduled four hours in my calendar each day to write. Because this was a very important project for me I decided at the outset that nothing short of my office being on fire was going to interfere with the time I allocated.

- The Criteria:

Break large projects into specific tasks that can be completed in a set period of time. In the dog training world we would say, "split don't lump!"

- Allocate Time:

Rather than trying to schedule the entire project all at once set times to complete the specific pieces. Schedule them when you function best. If you are a night owl, then do not schedule them at 7 a.m. Most of my creative work is done late at night as I function well then.

- Plan Action:

Now, get it done. Begin each task when you have it scheduled. Don't procrastinate. Once it is completed, you will feel a huge sense of accomplishment. Congratulations!

© Can Stock Photo Inc. / ewastudio

"If the first thing you do each morning is to eat a live frog, you can go through the day with the satisfaction of knowing that that is probably the worst thing that is going to happen to you all day long!"- Mark Twain

References

Beard, C., & Wilson, J.P. (2013). Experiential Learning. A Handbook for Education, Training and Coaching. 3rd edn. London, UK: Kogan Page.

Chance, P. (2008). Learning and Behavior. Belmont, CA: Wadsworth Cengage Learning.

Covey, Stephen R. (2004). The 7 Habits of Highly Effective People: Restoring the Character Ethic. [Rev. ed.]. New York, NY: Free Press.

Davis, D. (2009). Controlling Training: Tips, Tools and Techniques for Effective on the Job Training. Lulu Publishing. Lulu.com.

Eisenhower, D. D. (1954). Address at the Second Assembly of the World Council of Churches, Evanston, Illinois. Available at:<http://www.presidency.ucsb.edu/ws/?pid=9991> [February 27, 2017].

Kerzner, H. (2001). Project Management. New York, NY: John Wiley & Sons Inc.

Kolb, D. A. (2015). Experiential Leaning. 2nd edn. Upper Saddle River, NJ: Pearson Education Inc.

Levy, L. (2014). How Stress Affects The Brain During Learning. Available at: <www.edudemic.com/stress-affects-brain-learning> [July 27, 2015].

Lindsay S. (2005). Applied Dog Behavior and Training, vol. 3. Oxford, UK: Blackwell Publishing.

Lindsay S. (2000). Applied Dog Behavior and Training, vol. 1. Oxford, UK: Blackwell Publishing.

McCarthy, B., & McCarthy D. (2006). Teaching Around the 4MAT Cycle. Thousand Oaks, CA: Corwin Press.

Miltenberger, R.G. (2004). Behavior Modification Principles and Procedures. 3rd edn. Belmont, CA: Thompson.

Mullins, L.J. (2002). Management and Organizational Behavior Edinburgh, UK: Pearson Education Ltd.

O'Heare, J. (2007). Aggressive Behavior in Dogs. Ottawa, ON: Publishing.

O'Heare, J. (2004). Canine Neuropsychology. 3rd edn. Ottawa, ON: Publishing.

Pande, S., Neuman, R.P., & Cavanagh, R.R. (2000). The Six Sigma Way: How GE, Motorola, and Other Top Companies are Honing Their Performance. New York, NY: McGraw Hill.

Paul, R. (2008). The Logic of Creative and Critical Thinking. Available at: <www.criticalthinking.org> [August 15, 2015].

Pierce, D. W., & Cheney, C.D. (2004). Behavior Analysis and Learning. Mahwah, NJ: Lawrence Erlbaum Associates, Inc.

Pollice, G. (2003). Teaching versus Training. *The Rational Edge Publication*. Available at:<www.ibm.com/developerworks/rational/library/content/Rational Edge/mar04/3810.pdf> [August 15, 2015].

Rao, M.S. (2008). Teaching versus Training. Available from:

<www.profmsr.blogspot.com/2008/08/teaching-vs-training.html> [August 15, 2015].

Squire, L. R. (2004). Memory Systems of the brain: A brief history and current perspective. *Science Direct*. Available at: <www.amyalexander.wiki.westga.edu/file/view/memory+systems.pdf> [August 15, 2015]

Wolvin, A.D. (1983). Improving Listening Skills. In *Improving Speaking and Listening Skills. New Directions for College Learning Assistance*. Rubin, R. B. (Ed.), vol. 12. San Francisco, CA: Jossey- Bass, Inc.

About Niki Tudge

Niki Tudge PCBC-A, CDBC, CDT, DipABT (Diploma Animal Behavior Technology) DipCBST (Diploma Canine Behavior Science and Technology), Certified People Trainer, HCITB, TS1, TS2 & TS3. Certified Facilitator - Acuity Institute.

Passionate about training and developing people, Niki is certified through both the HCITB and Acuity Institute. She also holds multiple credentials for animal behavior and training with years of academic and hands on experience creating, developing and growing small businesses. Jack of much and master of few, Niki is a proud founding member of #BillyNoMates!

Acknowledgments

I have dedicated the last 5 years of my professional career to the Pet Professional Guild, DogSmith and DogNostics eLearning to bring together like-minded pet professionals so we can further engage, educate and empower pet owners, helping them to make educated and informed decisions on behalf of their pets. I sincerely hope this resource helps you to do just that in a more strategic and effective manner.

As with all of my projects there are people behind the scenes working hard with little or no recognition. For you, thank you for your support and encouragement. Many thanks and much appreciation to Susan Nilson for so diligently editing and reediting this book. Susan is always an absolute pleasure to work with. It was hugely beneficial to have her on my team, not only as an excellent copy editor but also as a Professional Canine Behavior Consultant she is uniquely equipped to help question and flesh out concepts. To all of you #BillyNoMates whether you know if it not you played a part in this effort!

Finally, thank you to Rick Ingram for putting all of my concepts into really effective graphics making it easier to understand.

Sponsored by The Dogsmith and DogNostics eLearning

1.888.DogSmith (364-7648)

ISBN 978-163535595-6

www.ingramcontent.com/pod-product-compliance
Lightning Source LLC
Chambersburg PA
CBHW052059070526
44584CB00017B/2257